SPECTRUM

Spelling

Grade 1

Published by Spectrum
an imprint of Carson-Dellosa Publishing LLC
Greensboro, NC

Spectrum
An imprint of Carson-Dellosa Publishing LLC
P.O. Box 35665
Greensboro, NC 27425 USA

Printed in the USA • All rights reserved.   ISBN 978-0-7696-4261-1

04-304117811

Table of Contents Grade 1

Table of Contents, continued

Sounds and Spellings

The short **a** sound: b**a**g, d**a**d

The short **e** sound: b**e**d, h**e**n

The short **i** sound: p**i**g, **i**s

The short **o** sound: p**o**t, b**o**x

The short **u** sound: s**u**n, t**u**b

The long **a** sound: m**a**k**e**, d**a**y

The long **e** sound: m**e**, s**ee**, f**ee**t

The long **i** sound: l**i**k**e**, m**y**

The long **o** sound: h**o**m**e**, n**o**

The /k/ sound: **c**at, **k**ite, bla**ck**

The /cl/ sound: **cl**ap, **cl**ass

The /fl/ sound: **fl**ag, **fl**y

The /sn/ sound: **sn**ap, **sn**ug

The /st/ sound: **st**op, **st**em

The /wh/ sound: **wh**en, **wh**ite

The /sh/ sound: **sh**ut, **sh**ip

Lesson 1 The Letters I, L, T, K, Y, Z, V, W, and X

Say each letter. Trace each letter. Write each letter.

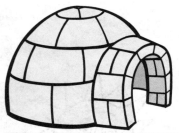

Lesson 1 The Letters **I**, **L**, **T**, **K**, **Y**, **Z**, **V**, **W**, and **X**

Say each letter. Trace each letter. Write each letter.

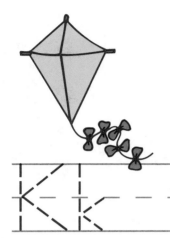

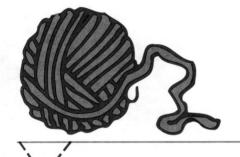

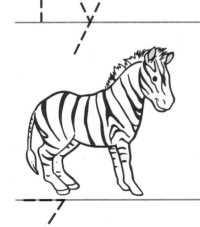

Lesson 1 The Letters **I**, **L**, **T**, **K**, **Y**, **Z**, **V**, **W**, and **X**

Say each letter. Trace each letter. Write each letter.

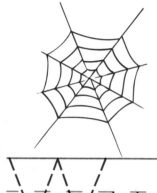

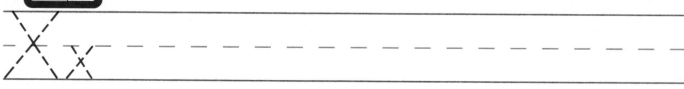

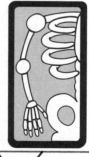

Lesson 1 The Letters I, L, T, K, Y, Z, V, W, and X

Draw lines to match the letters.

I   k   V   K   w

Z   T   I   Y   W

     i   y

X   x

    t   z   v   L

Circle the letters on each line that are the same.

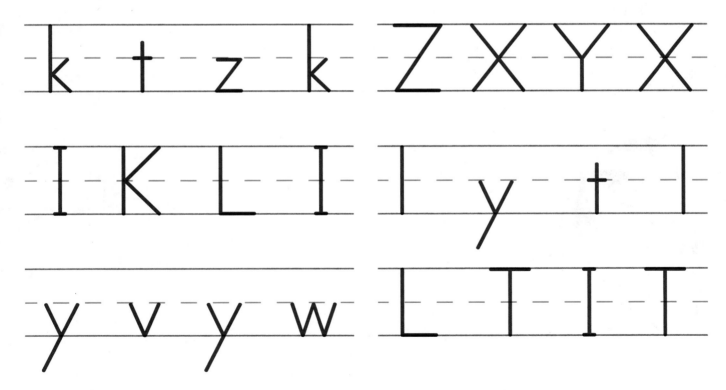

k t z k   Z X Y X

I K L I   l y t

y v y w   L T I T

Lesson 2 The Letters **O**, **C**, **U**, **S**, **J**, **G**, **P**, **B**, and **D**

Say each letter. Trace each letter. Write each letter.

O o – – – – – – – – – – – – – – – – –

C c – – – – – – – – – – – – – – – – –

U u – – – – – – – – – – – – – – – – –

Lesson 2 The Letters **O**, **C**, **U**, **S**, **J**, **G**, **P**, **B**, and **D**

Say each letter. Trace each letter. Write each letter.

S s _____

J j _____

G g _____

NAME _____

Lesson 2   The Letters O, C, U, S, J, G, P, B, and D

Say each letter. Trace each letter. Write each letter.

P p

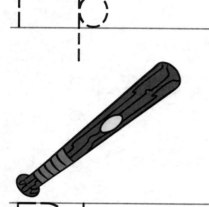

B b

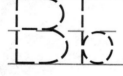

D d

NAME _____

Lesson 2 The Letters O, C, U, S, J, G, P, B, and D

Find the letters O, C, U, S, J, G, P, B, and D. Circle each letter.

Lesson 3 The Letters **H**, **M**, **N**, **A**, **E**, **Q**, **R**, and **F**

Say each letter. Trace each letter. Write each letter.

Lesson 3 The Letters **H**, **M**, **N**, **A**, **E**, **Q**, **R**, and **F**

Say each letter. Trace each letter. Write each letter.

A a _____

E e _____

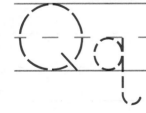

Q q _____

Lesson 3 The Letters **H**, **M**, **N**, **A**, **E**, **Q**, **R**, and **F**

Say each letter. Trace each letter. Write each letter.

R r

F f

Trace each word. Write each word.

fan

ham

Lesson 3 The Letters H, M, N, A, E, Q, R, and F

Find the letters **h**, **m**, **n**, **a**, **e**, **q**, **r**, and **f**. Circle each letter.

monkeys

squirrel

giraffe

elephants

reindeer

foxes

Lesson 4 The /t/, /m/, /s/, /j/, and /k/ Sounds at the Beginnings of Words

Name each picture. Circle the letter for the beginning sounds.

t   m   s   j   c

t j c	s t m	t j s
c m j	m t s	c j m
t c s	s c m	c m t

Lesson 4 The /t/, /m/, /s/, /j/, and /k/ Sounds at the Beginnings of Words

Name the pictures. Circle the pictures in each row with the same beginning sound. Write the letter for the beginning sound.

_____

_____

 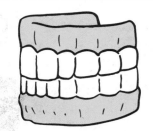 

_____

_____

_____

Lesson 4 The /t/, /m/, /s/, /j/, and /k/ Sounds at the Beginnings of Words

Name each picture. Write the letter for the beginning sound.

t m s j c

Lesson 4 The /t/, /m/, /s/, /j/, and /k/ Sounds at the Beginnings of Words

Name each picture. Write the letter for the beginning sound. Circle the correct word.

_____ __ __ _____

mop

top

_____ __ __ _____

jar

car

_____ __ __ _____

map

cap

_____ __ __ _____

six

mix

_____ __ __ _____

mat

cat

Lesson 5 The /d/, /f/, /g/, /n/, and /w/ Sounds at the Beginnings of Words

Name each picture. Circle the letter for the beginning sound.

d f g n w

d g w	w f n	n g d
d g f	g d n	n w d
g n d	d f g	w n g

Lesson 5 The /d/, /f/, /g/, /n/, and /w/ Sounds at the Beginnings of Words

Name the pictures. Circle the pictures in each row with the same beginning sound. Write the letter for the beginning sound.

Lesson 5 The /d/, /f/, /g/, /n/, and /w/ Sounds at the Beginnings of Words

Name each picture. Write the letter for the beginning sound.

d f g n w

Lesson 5 The /d/, /f/, /g/, /n/, and /w/ Sounds at the Beginnings of Words

Name each picture. Write the letter for the beginning sound. Then, circle the correct word. Write the correct word.

_____ fog _____

_____ dog _____

_____ wet _____

_____ net _____

_____ date _____

_____ gate _____

_____ wig _____

_____ dig _____

_____ wish _____

_____ fish _____

Lesson 6 The /b/, /h/, /p/, and /r/ Sounds at the Beginnings of Words

Name each picture. Circle the letter for the beginning sound.

b h p r

b h p	r b p	h p b
r p h	h p b	b h r
r h b	r p b	p h r

Lesson 6 The /b/, /h/, /p/, and /r/ Sounds at the Beginnings of Words

Name the pictures. Circle the pictures in each row with the same beginning sound. Write the letter for the beginning sound.

NAME _____

Lesson 6 The /b/, /h/, /p/, and /r/ Sounds at the Beginnings of Words

Name each picture. Write the letter for the beginning sound.

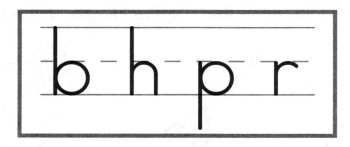

 ___

 ___

 ___

 ___

 ___

 ___

 ___

 ___

 ___

 ___

Lesson 6 The /b/, /h/, /p/, and /r/ Sounds at the Beginnings of Words

Name each picture. Write the letter for the beginning sound. Circle the correct word.

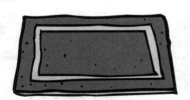

____ ____

big

pig

____ ____

hat

bat

____ ____

hen

pen

____ ____

bug

rug

____ ____

hall

ball

Lesson 7 The /k/, /l/, /v/, /y/, and /z/ Sounds at the Beginnings of Words

Name each picture. Circle the letter for the beginning sound.

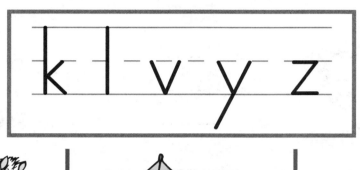

		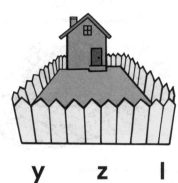
l y z	**k l v**	**y z l**

l k v	**z v y**	**y k z**

l z k	**y k v**	**y k l**

Lesson 7 The /k/, /l/, /v/, /y/, and /z/ Sounds at the Beginnings of Words

Name the pictures. Circle the pictures in each row with the same beginning sound. Write the letter for the beginning sound.

Lesson 7 The /k/, /l/, /v/, /y/, and /z/ Sounds at the Beginnings of Words

Name each picture. Write the letter for the beginning sound.

k l v y z

Lesson 7 The /k/, /l/, /v/, /y/, and /z/ Sounds at the Beginnings of Words

Name each picture. Write the letter for the beginning sound. Then, circle the correct word. Write the correct word.

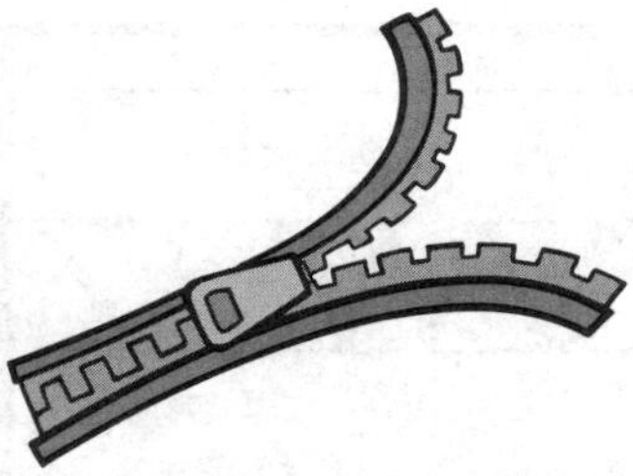

_____ zip
_____ lip
_____

_____ list
_____ kiss
_____

_____ yarn
_____ barn
_____

_____ vine
_____ line
_____

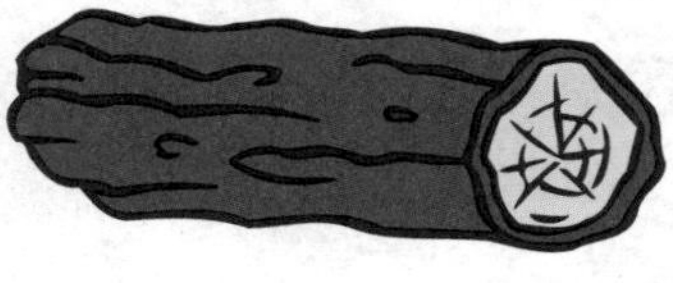

_____ log
_____ cog
_____

Review Lessons 1–7

Name each picture. Write the letter for the beginning sound. Circle the correct word.

bcdfgh jklmnprstvwyz

1.    _ _ _ _   **hat**

   _ _ _ _   **cat**

2.    _ _ _ _   **car**

   _ _ _ _   **jar**

3.    _ _ _ _   **log**

   _ _ _ _   **dog**

4.    _ _ _ _   **meal**

   _ _ _ _   **seal**

5.    _ _ _ _   **fox**

   _ _ _ _   **box**

Review Lessons 1–7

6.  _____ _ _ _____   nest

vest

7.  _____ _ _ _____   barn

yarn

8.  _____ _ _ _____   top

mop

9.  _____ _ _ _____   sock

lock

10.  _____ _ _ _____   man

van

11.  _____ _ _ _____   ring

king

Lesson 8 The /d/, /t/, and /m/ Sounds at the Ends of Words

Name each picture. Circle the letter for the ending sound.

d t m	t d m	m t d
d t m	d m t	m t d
d t m	t m d	m d t

Lesson 8 The /d/, /t/, and /m/ Sounds at the Ends of Words

Name the pictures. Circle the pictures in each row with the same ending sound. Write the letter for the ending sound.

Lesson 8 The /d/, /t/, and /m/ Sounds at the Ends of Words

Name each picture. Write the letter for the ending sound.

d t m

Lesson 8 The /d/, /t/, and /m/ Sounds at the Ends of Words

Name each picture. Write the letter for the ending sound. Circle the correct word.

_____
_ _
_____

ham

hat

_____
_ _
_____

ram

rat

_____
_ _
_____

pot

pod

_____
_ _
_____

bad

bed

_____
_ _
_____

food

foot

Lesson 9 The /s/, /g/, and /b/ Sounds at the Ends of Words

Name each picture. Circle the letter for the ending sound.

		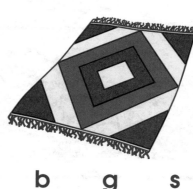
s **g** b	**g** s b	b **g** s

s b g	b **g** s	s g **b**

b g s	g b **s**	s g **b**

Lesson 9 The /s/, /g/, and /b/ Sounds at the Ends of Words

Name the pictures. Circle the pictures in each row with the same ending sound. Write the letter for the ending sound.

Lesson 9 The /s/, /g/, and /b/ Sounds at the Ends of Words

Name each picture. Write the letter for the ending sound.

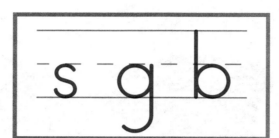

 _____

 _____

 _____

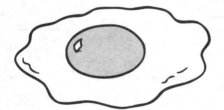 _____

 _____

 _____

 _____

 _____

 _____

 _____

 _____

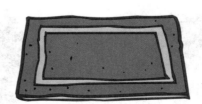 _____

Lesson 9 The /s/, /g/, and /b/ Sounds at the Ends of Words

Name each picture. Write the letter for the ending sound. Circle the correct word.

_____
_ _
_____

tub

tug

_____
_ _
_____

bus

bug

_____
_ _
_____

rub

rug

_____
_ _
_____

bib

big

_____
_ _
_____

grab

gas

Lesson 10 The /p/, /n/, and /x/ Sounds at the Ends of Words

Name each picture. Circle the letter for the ending sound.

p n x

p   n   x   n   p   x   x   n   p

n   x   p   p   x   n   x   n   p

n   p   x   p   x   n   n   x   p

Lesson 10 The /p/, /n/, and /x/ Sounds at the Ends of Words

Name the pictures. Circle the pictures in each row with the same ending sound. Write the letter for the ending sound.

Lesson 10 The /p/, /n/, and /x/ Sounds at the Ends of Words

Name each picture. Write the letter for the ending sound.

p n x

Lesson 10 The /p/, /n/, and /x/ Sounds at the Ends of Words

Name each picture. Write the letter for the ending sound. Circle the correct word.

map
man

ox
on

cap
can

six
sip

fax
fan

Review Lessons 8–10

Name each picture. Write the letter for the ending sound. Circle the correct word.

b d g m n p s t x

1.  ___ ___

   pin

   pig

2.  ___ ___

   fog

   fox

3.  ___ ___

   bus

   bug

4.  ___ ___

   man

   map

5.  ___ ___

   bed

   beg

Review Lessons 8–10

6.  _____

      — —

      _____

ham

hat

7.  _____

      — —

      _____

plug

plum

8.  _____

      — —

      _____

rug

rub

9.  _____

      — —

      _____

pat

pan

10.  _____

      — —

      _____

sip

six

11.  _____

      — —

      _____

clam

clap

Lesson 11 The Short **a** Sound

Say **hat**.

Name each picture. Listen for the short **a** sound as in **hat**. Circle the pictures with the short **a** sound.

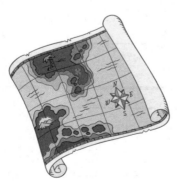

Lesson 11 The Short **a** Sound

Name each picture. Listen for the short **a** sound. Circle the pictures with the short **a** sound.

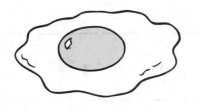

NAME _____

Lesson 11 The Short **a** Sound

Name each picture. Listen for the short **a** sound.
Write **a** on the line if you hear the short **a** sound.

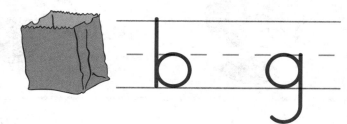

a

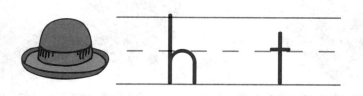 h ___ t

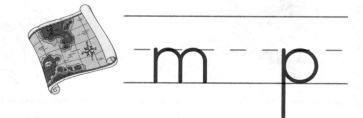 b ___ g

 p ___ n

 m ___ p

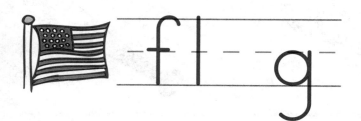 f l ___ g

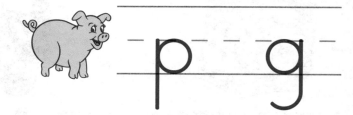 v ___ n

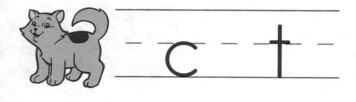 c ___ t

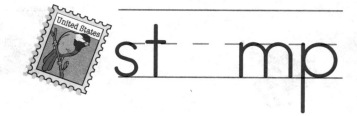 p ___ g

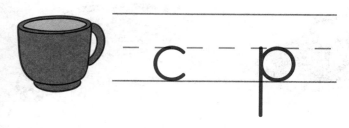 c ___ p

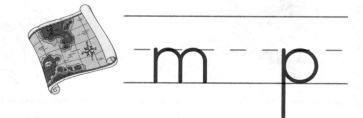 st ___ mp

Lesson 11 The Short a Sound

Name each picture. Circle the correct word. Write the correct word.

cap

cup

_____

- - - - - - - - - -

_____

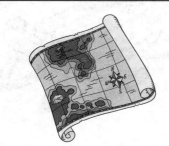

mop

map

_____

- - - - - - - - - -

_____

pin

pan

_____

- - - - - - - - - -

_____

fan

fin

_____

- - - - - - - - - -

_____

bug

bag

_____

- - - - - - - - - -

_____

Lesson 12 The Short i Sound

Say **pin**.

Name each picture. Listen for the short **i** sound as in **pin**. Circle the pictures with the short **i** sound.

NAME _____

Lesson 12 The Short i Sound

Name the pictures. Listen for the short **i** sound. Circle the pictures in each row with the short **i** sound.

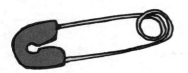  

Lesson 12   The Short i Sound

Name each picture. Listen for the short **i** sound.
Write **i** on the line if you hear the short **i** sound.

_i_

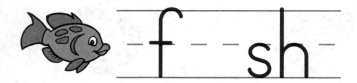 f ___ sh

 b ___ b

 cr ___ b

 s ___ d

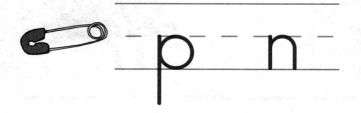 p ___ n

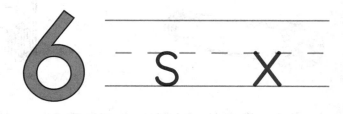 s ___ x

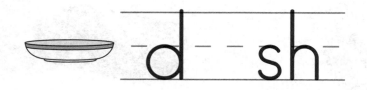 d ___ sh

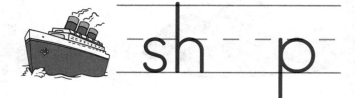 sh ___ p

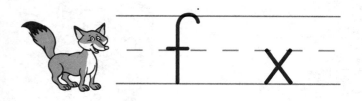 f ___ x

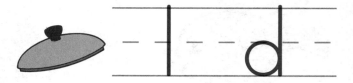 l ___ d

Lesson 12 The Short i Sound

Name each picture. Circle the correct word. Write the correct word.

hall

hill

_____

- - - - - - - -

_____

pin

pan

_____

- - - - - - - -

_____

crib

crab

_____

- - - - - - - -

_____

wig

wag

_____

- - - - - - - -

_____

clap

clip

_____

- - - - - - - -

_____

Lesson 13 The Short o Sound

Say **top**.

Name each picture. Listen for the short **o** sound as in **top**. Circle the pictures with the short **o** sound.

Lesson 13 The Short o Sound

Name the pictures. Listen for the short o sound. Circle the pictures in each row with the short o sound.

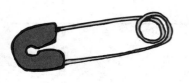  

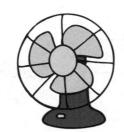 

Lesson 13 The Short o Sound

Name each picture. Listen for the short o sound.
Write o on the line if you hear the short o sound.

o

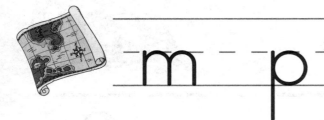 m ___ p

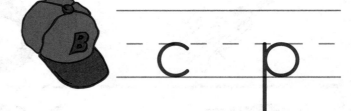 c ___ p

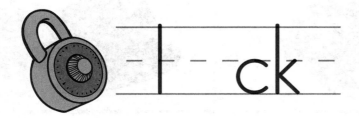 l ___ ck

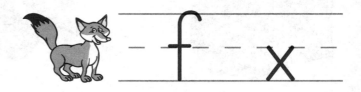 f ___ x

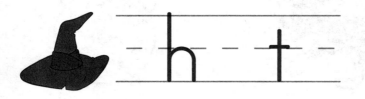 h ___ t

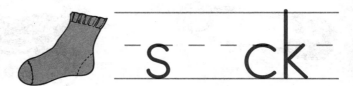 s ___ ck

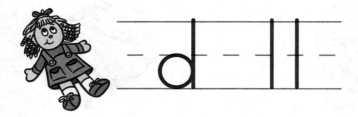 d ___ ll

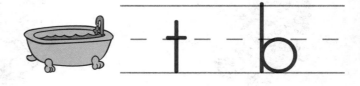 t ___ b

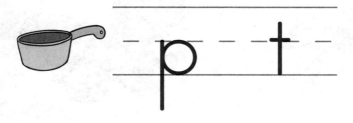 p ___ t

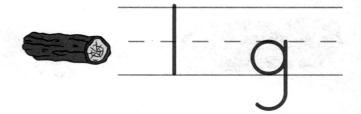 l ___ g

Lesson 13 The Short o Sound

Name each picture. Circle the correct word. Write the correct word.

map

mop

_____

- - - - - - - - -

_____

lock

luck

_____

- - - - - - - - -

_____

sack

sock

_____

- - - - - - - - -

_____

pot

pit

_____

- - - - - - - - -

_____

dull

doll

_____

- - - - - - - - -

_____

Lesson 14 The Short **u** Sound

Say **cup**.

Name each picture. Listen for the short **u** sound as in **cup**. Circle the pictures with the short **u** sound.

Lesson 14 The Short u Sound

Name the pictures. Listen for the short **u** sound. Circle the pictures in each row with the short **u** sound.

Lesson 14 The Short u Sound

Name each picture. Listen for the short **u** sound.
Write **u** on the line if you hear the short **u** sound.

u

 d __ ck    n __ t

 s __ n   c __ p

 b __ ll    f __ sh

 fr __ g    b __ s

 t __ b    b __ g

Lesson 14 The Short **u** Sound

Name each picture. Circle the correct word. Write the correct word.

deck
_____

duck
_____

bug
_____

bag
_____

cup
_____

cap
_____

trick
_____

truck
_____

net
_____

nut
_____

NAME _____

Lesson 15 The Short e Sound

Say **bell**.

Name the pictures. Listen for the short **e** sound as in **bell**. Circle the pictures with the short **e** sound.

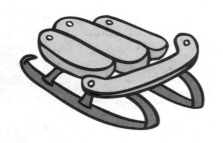

Lesson 15 The Short e Sound

Name the pictures. Listen for the short **e** sound. Circle the pictures in each row with the short **e** sound.

Lesson 15 The Short **e** Sound

Name each picture. Listen for the short **e** sound.
Write **e** on the line if you hear the short **e** sound.

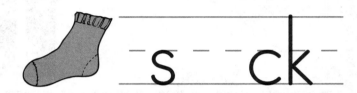 e

 b __ d   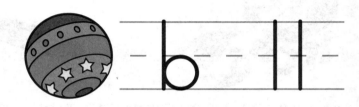 s __ ck

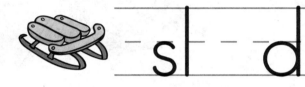 s l __ d   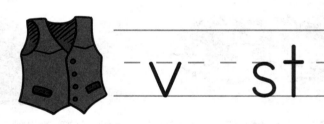 b __ ll

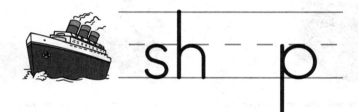 sh __ p   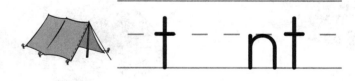 v __ st

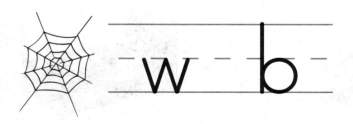 t __ nt    f l __ g

w __ b   **10** t __ n

Lesson 15 The Short e Sound

Name each picture. Circle the correct word. Write the correct word.

bell

ball

_____

- - - - - - - - -

_____

nut

net

_____

- - - - - - - - -

_____

bad

bed

_____

- - - - - - - - -

_____

10

ten

tin

_____

- - - - - - - - -

_____

pin

pen

_____

- - - - - - - - -

_____

Review Lessons 11–15

Name the first picture in each row. Name the other pictures. Circle the picture with the same middle sound as the first picture. Write the letter of the middle sound.

Review Lessons 11–15

Name each picture. Write the letter for the middle sound. Circle the word that names the picture.

‾‾‾‾‾
– –
‾‾‾‾‾

deck
duck
dock

‾‾‾‾‾
– –
‾‾‾‾‾

bell
bull
ball

‾‾‾‾‾
– –
‾‾‾‾‾

net
nut
not

‾‾‾‾‾
– –
‾‾‾‾‾

sack
sock
sick

‾‾‾‾‾
– –
‾‾‾‾‾

hill
hall
hull

Lesson 16 Words with the Short **a** Sound

Spelling Words

Say each word. Listen for the short **a** sound. Trace each word.
Write the word.

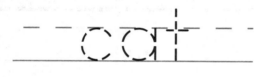

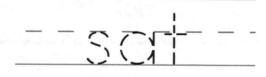

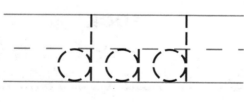

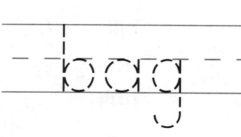

Lesson 16 Words with the Short **a** Sound

Words in Context

Write the missing spelling words.

_____

– – – – – – – – –

My _____ jumped out of the tree.

_____

– – – – – – – – –

It _____ to the van with me.

_____

– – – – – – – – –

We _____ in the back of the van.

_____   _____

– – – – – – – –   – – – – – – – –

My _____ had my soccer _____.

_____

– – – – – – – – – –

We will go as soon as we _____.

Word Building

Write the letter to make words with the short **a** sound.

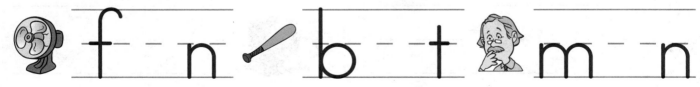

f _ _ n   _ _ b _ _ t   m _ _ n

Lesson 16 Words with the Short **a** Sound

Fun with Words

Find the spelling words.
Look across and down.
Circle each one.

c	s	r	e	b
o	d	a	d	c
r	s	n	o	a
c	a	t	i	n
g	t	b	a	g

Words Across the Curriculum

Say each science word. Trace each word. Then, write each word.

gas   hand   sand

Write each science word
next to the picture it names.

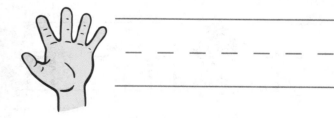

Lesson 16 Words with the Short **a** Sound

Words in Writing

Write about a time you went to a park.
Use at least two words from the box.

| ran | can | cat | sat | dad | bag | gas | sand | hand |

_____

_ _

_____

_____

_____

Dictionary Practice

Write the word in each row that comes first in ABC order.

_____

_ _ _ _ _ _ _ _ _ _ _ _ _ _ _ _ _

cat   sat   bag   _____

_____

_ _ _ _ _ _ _ _ _ _ _ _ _ _ _ _ _

gas   can   ran   _____

_____

_ _ _ _ _ _ _ _ _ _ _ _ _ _ _ _ _

sand   dad   hand   _____

NAME _____

Lesson 17 Words with the Short i Sound

Spelling Words

Say each word. Listen for the short **i** sound. Trace each word.
Write the word.

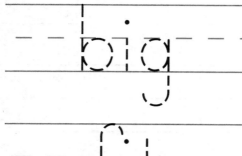

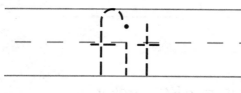

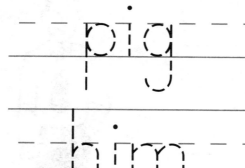

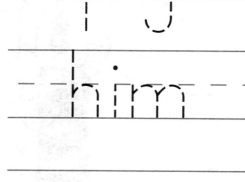

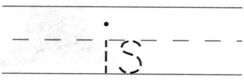

Lesson 17   Words with the Short i Sound

Words in Context
Write the missing spelling words.

_____

‑ ‑ ‑ ‑ ‑ ‑ ‑ ‑

I have a pet _____.

_____

‑ ‑ ‑ ‑ ‑ ‑ ‑ ‑   ‑ ‑ ‑ ‑ ‑ ‑ ‑

He _____ pink, and very, very _____.

_____   _____

‑ ‑ ‑ ‑ ‑ ‑ ‑ ‑   ‑ ‑ ‑ ‑ ‑ ‑ ‑

I _____ call _____ Tiny Tim.

_____

‑ ‑ ‑ ‑ ‑ ‑ ‑ ‑

But that name does not _____.

Word Building
Write the letter to make words with the short i sound.

 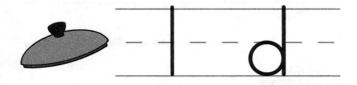 s t

 d sh

l d

 b b

Lesson 17 Words with the Short i Sound

Fun with Words

Say each word. Write the spelling word or words that rhyme with each word.

sit _____   rim _____   hid _____

fizz _____   jig _____, _____

Words Across the Curriculum

Say each science word. Trace each word. Then, write each word.

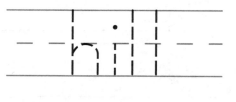   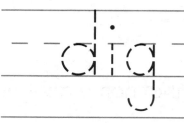

Write each science word
next to the picture it names.

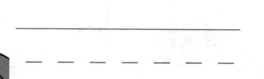   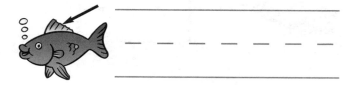

Lesson 17 Words with the Short i Sound

Words in Writing

Write about what a farm is like. Use at least two words from the box.

| did | big | fit | pig | him | is | fin | hill | dig |

_____

_ _

_____

_ _

_____

Misspelled Words

Circle the four misspelled words. Write the words correctly on the lines below.

   Did you see the pigg on the farm? I saw hem last week. He iz very beg. He needs a new pen.

_____   _____

_ _ _ _ _ _ _ _ _ _ _ _ _   _ _ _ _ _ _ _ _ _ _ _ _ _

_____   _____

_ _ _ _ _ _ _ _ _ _ _ _ _   _ _ _ _ _ _ _ _ _ _ _ _ _

_____   _____

Lesson 18 Words with the Short o Sound

Spelling Words

Say each word. Listen for the short **o** sound. Trace each word.
Write the word.

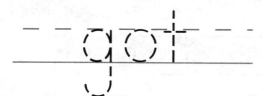

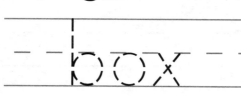

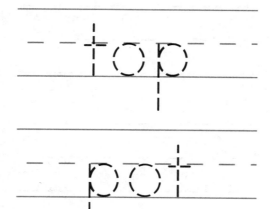

Lesson 18 Words with the Short o Sound

Words in Context

Write the missing spelling words.

_____

— — — — — — — -

My _____ made a snack.

_____

— — — — — — — -

She put a _____ of soup on the stove. She put the

_____   _____

— — — — — — — —   — — — — — — — —

lid on _____. She _____ out a

_____   _____

— — — — — — — —   — — — — — — — —

_____ of crackers. I did _____.

have to help!

Word Building

Name each picture. Write the letter of the beginning sound.

 OX

 ock

 op

Lesson 18 Words with the Short o Sound

Fun with Words

Look at the letters on the blocks. Use
the letters to make the spelling words.

_____   _____   _____

_ _ _ _ _ _ _ _ _ _   _ _ _ _ _ _ _ _ _ _   _ _ _ _ _ _ _ _ _ _

_____   _____   _____

_____   _____   _____

Words Across the Curriculum

Say each social studies word. Trace each word. Then, write each word.

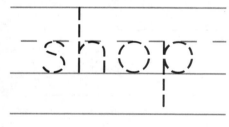   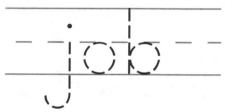   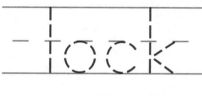

_ _ _ _ _ _ _ _ _ _   _ _ _ _ _ _ _ _ _ _   _ _ _ _ _ _ _ _ _ _

Write each social studies word next to its meaning.

_____   _____   _____

_ _ _ _ _ _   _ _ _ _ _ _   _ _ _ _ _ _

close _____   store _____   work _____

Lesson 18 Words with the Short o Sound

Words in Writing

Write about what your mom or dad likes to do. Use at least three words from the box.

| got | box | mom | not | top | pot | shop | job | lock |

_____

_ _ _ _ _ _ _ _ _ _ _ _ _ _ _ _ _ _ _

_____

_ _ _ _ _ _ _ _ _ _ _ _ _ _ _ _ _ _ _

_____

_ _ _ _ _ _ _ _ _ _ _ _ _ _ _ _ _ _ _

_____

Dictionary Practice

Write the missing letters in ABC order.

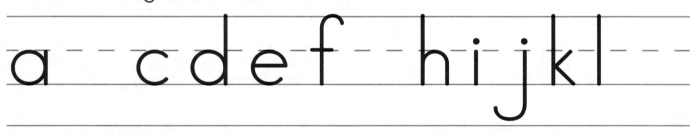

a c d e f h i j k l

n p q s u v w y z

NAME _____

Lesson 19 Words with the Short **u** Sound

Spelling Words

Say each word. Listen for the short **u** sound. Trace each word.
Write the word.

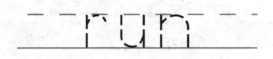

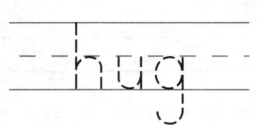

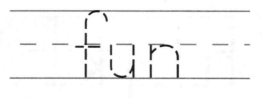

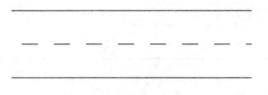

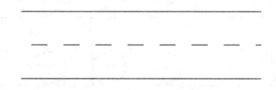

Lesson 19 Words with the Short **u** Sound

Words in Context
Write the missing spelling words.

_____

_ _ _ _ _ _ _ _

Do you like to _____ on the beach? It's

_____   _____

_ _ _ _ _ _ _ _ _ _   _ _ _ _ _ _ _ _ _

_____! The sand seems to _____

_____

_ _ _ _ _ _ _ _ _

your feet, _____ they still feel

_____

_ _ _ _ _ _ _ _

free. The _____ is warm on your

_____

_ _ _ _ _ _ _

body. The sea is much better than a bath in a _____.

Word Building
Name each picture. Write the letter of the ending sound.

 cu    ru    bu

Lesson 19 Words with the Short **u** Sound

Fun with Words

Look at each row of letters. There is a spelling word hidden in each row. Circle the word. Then, write it.

f a e f u n t u _____   u s t h u g h b _____

t s h f h b u t _____   n o s u n u g b _____

Words Across the Curriculum

Say each science word. Trace each word. Then, write each word.

_____   _____   _____

_____   _____   _____

Write each science word
next to the picture it names.

Lesson 19 Words with the Short **u** Sound

Words in Writing

Write about something you do
that is fun. Use at least two words
from the box.

run	sun	fun	nut	mud
hug	but	tub	cub	

_____

- - - - - - - - - - - - - - -

_____

- - - - - - - - - - - - - - -

_____

Misspelled Words

Circle the four misspelled words. Then, write the sentence and spell
the words correctly.

It's fune to runn in the sen, bot then you need a bath.

_____

- - - - - - - - - - - - - - -

_____

- - - - - - - - - - - - - - -

_____

Lesson 20 Words with the Short **e** Sound

Spelling Words

Say each word. Listen for the short **e** sound. Trace each word.
Write the word.

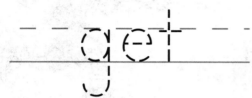

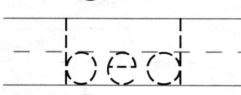

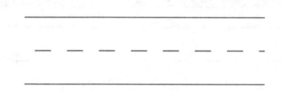

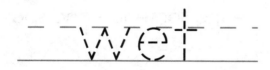

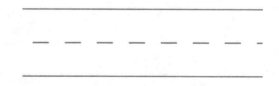

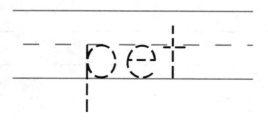

Lesson 20 Words with the Short **e** Sound

Words in Context

Write the missing spelling words.

I have a funny _____. She sleeps on a nest instead

of a bed. Can you guess what she is? _____, she's

a _____. She likes to _____

_____, so she swims

in the pond.

Word Building

Name each picture. Write the
letter of the beginning sound.

 eg

 et

10 en

Lesson 20 Words with the Short e Sound

Fun with Words

Name each picture. Write the spelling word that has the same beginning sound.

Words Across the Curriculum

Say each science word. Trace each word. Then, write each word.

egg   stem   web

Write the science word
that goes with each clue.

a spider's home _____

part of a flower _____   found in a nest _____

Lesson 20 Words with the Short e Sound

Words in Writing

Write about a pet you would like to have.
Use at least three words from the box.

get	yes	hen	egg	web
bed	wet	pet	stem	

_____

_ _

_____

_____

_____

_ _

Dictionary Practice

Write the spelling words in ABC order.

get	yes	hen
bed	wet	pet

1. _____

2. _____

3. _____

4. _____

5. _____

6. _____

Review Lessons 16–20

ran	did	got	run	get
can	big	box	hug	bed
cat	fit	mom	sun	yes
sat	pig	not	but	wet
dad	him	top	fun	hen
bag	is	pot	tub	pet

Write the spelling word that means the opposite.

no _____

small _____

dad _____

dry _____

her _____

Write the spelling word that rhymes.

nut _____

fox _____

rub _____

men _____

lit _____

Review Lessons 16-20

Write the spelling word that goes with each pair of words.

kiss, love _____   tiger, lion _____

bottom, side _____   sleep, blanket _____

cow, hen _____

Write the spelling word that fits in each sentence.

I can _____ fast.   The _____ is shining.

I _____ a new toy.   The _____ is on the stove.

It's _____ to go to the park.

Lesson 21 Words with **cl** and **fl**

Spelling Words

Say each word. Listen to the beginning sound. Trace each word.
Write the word.

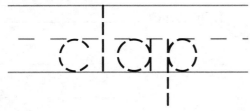

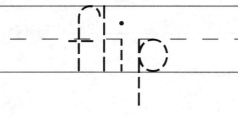

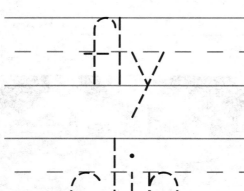

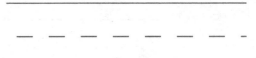

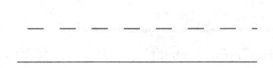

Lesson 21 Words with **cl** and **fl**

Words in Context

Write each spelling word next to the picture it names.

 _____

 _____

 _____

 _____

 _____

 _____

Word Building

Write **cl** or **fl** to make words.

 _____ower

  _____ock

 _____oud

Lesson 21 Words with **cl** and **fl**

Fun with Words

Find the spelling words. Look across and down. Circle each one.

k	c	f	l	a	t	c
u	c	l	g	t	b	l
c	l	a	m	f	y	i
k	a	g	s	l	e	p
u	p	n	g	i	p	u
b	f	l	y	p	t	y

Words Across the Curriculum

Say each social studies word. Trace each word. Then, write each word.

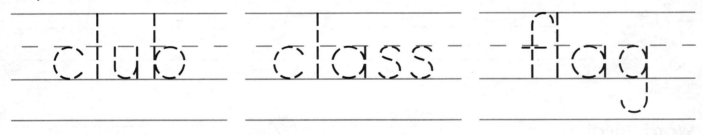

Write each social studies word next to the word with the same ending.

bag _____   grass _____   tub _____

Lesson 21   Words with cl and fl

Words in Writing

Write two tongue-twisters. Use at least two words from the box.

| clap | flat | clam | flip | fly | clip | club | class | flag |

_____

_ _

_____

_ _

_____

Misspelled Words

Circle the four misspelled words. Then, write words correctly on the lines below.

   Have you ever done a flep into a pool? You fli over the flatt water. You close up your body like a clem. Then, you splash into the water.

_____   _____

_ _ _ _ _ _ _ _ _ _ _ _   _ _ _ _ _ _ _ _ _ _ _ _

_____   _____

_ _ _ _ _ _ _ _ _ _ _ _   _ _ _ _ _ _ _ _ _ _ _ _

_____   _____

Lesson 22 Words with **sn** and **st**

Spelling Words

Say each word. Listen to the beginning sound. Trace each word.
Write the word.

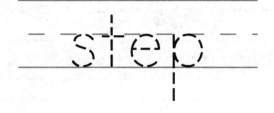

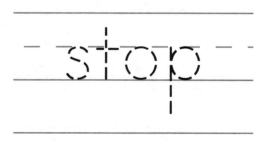

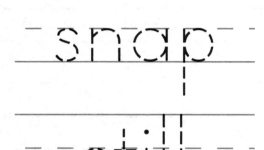

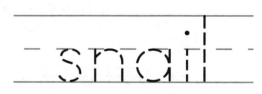

Lesson 22 Words with **sn** and **st**

Words in Context
Write the missing spelling words.

_____

_ _ _ _ _ _ _ _

I was warm and _____ in my tent. Then, I heard a twig

_____   _____

_ _ _ _ _ _ _ _ _ _   _ _ _ _ _ _

_____. I got up and took a _____

_____

_ _ _ _ _ _ _ _

outside. I saw a _____. It did not

_____   _____

_ _ _ _ _ _ _ _ _   _ _ _ _ _ _ _ _

_____ moving, but it _____

didn't go very fast.

Word Building
Write **s** to the end to make words
that mean more than one. Then,
write the new words.

_ _ _ _ _ _ _ _

_ _ _ _ _ _ _ _

snap_____ _____

_ _ _ _ _ _ _ _

_ _ _ _ _ _ _ _

step_____ _____   stop_____ _____

Lesson 22 Words with **sn** and **st**

Fun with Words

Write the spelling word that rhymes with each word.

hill _____ pail _____

bug _____ hop _____

Words Across the Curriculum

Say each science word. Then, write each word.

star   snow   snake

Write each science word next
to the picture it names.

Lesson 22 Words with **sn** and **st**

Words in Writing

Make up a story. Use at least three words from the box.

| step | snap | still | snail | stop | snug | star | snow | snake |

_____

- -

_____

- -

_____

- -

_____

- -

_____

- -

_____

Dictionary Practice

A **verb** is a word that tells what happens. Circle the verb in each sentence.

Please stop that dog!   Can you snap your fingers?

The snail moves slowly.   Did you step on the grass?

Lesson 23 Words with **ch** and **th**

Spelling Words

Say each word. Listen to the beginning sound. Trace each word.
Write the word.

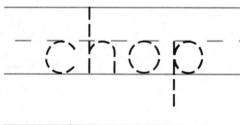

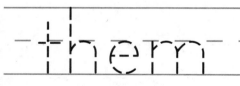

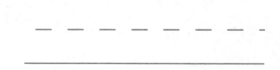

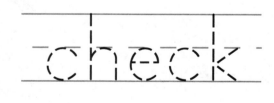

Lesson 23 Words with **ch** and **th**

Words in Context

Write the missing spelling words.

_____

— — — — — — — — — — —

_____ is how my dad makes soup. He will

_____   _____

— — — — — — — —   — — — — — — — —

_____ vegetables. _____, he will boil

_____   _____

— — — — — — — —   — — — — — — — —

_____. After an hour, my dad will _____

_____

— — — — — — — —

to see if his soup is done. Doesn't _____ sound easy?

Word Building

Add **ch** or **th** to make words that fit the meanings. Then, write the words.

_____   _____

talk with a friend ___  ___   _____

_____   _____

skinny ___ in ___   _____

Lesson 23 Words with **ch** and **th**

Fun with Words

Look at the letters on the balloons. Use
the letters to make the spelling words.

_____   _____

- - - - - - - - - - - -   - - - - - - - - - - - -

_____   _____

_____   _____

_____   _____

Words Across the Curriculum

Say each math word. Trace each word. Then, write each word.

_____   _____   _____

- - - - - - - - - - - -   - - - - - - - - - - - -   _____

_____

- - - - - - - - - - - -

Write the math word that ends like **with**.   _____

_____

- - - - - - - - - - - -

Write the math word that ends like **rich**.

Lesson 23 Words with **ch** and **th**

Words in Writing

Write directions telling how you do something. Use at least two words from the box.

| then | this | chop | them | check | that | math | chart | much |

_____

- -

_____

- -

_____

- -

_____

Misspelled Words

Circle the four misspelled words. Then, write the words correctly on the lines below.

Thes is how to add numbers. Make sure tat you write the numbers clearly. Thene, find the sum. Make sure you chec your answer.

_____   _____

- - - - - - - - - -   - - - - - - - - - -

_____   _____

- - - - - - - - - -   - - - - - - - - - -

_____   _____

Lesson 24 Words with **wh** and **sh**

Spelling Words

Say each word. Listen to the beginning sound. Trace each word.
Write the word.

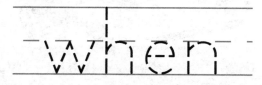

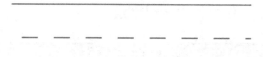

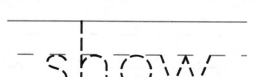

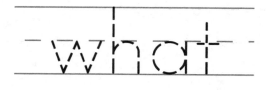

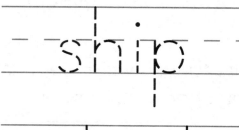

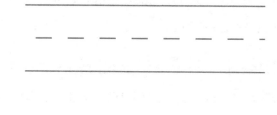

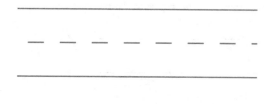

Lesson 24 Words with **wh** and **sh**

Words in Context

Write the missing spelling words.

_____

- - - - - - - -

_____ did you do last summer?

S.S. Fun Ship

_____

- - - - - - -

I sailed on a _____ where I had my own room. I could

_____   _____

- - - - - -   - - - - - -

_____ the door. _____ we go to the

_____   _____

- - - - - -   - - - - -

shore, I will _____ you _____ boat I was on.

Word Building

Add the letters **wh** to make words that ask questions. Remember, sentences start with a capital letter.

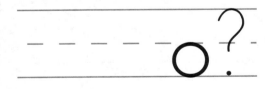

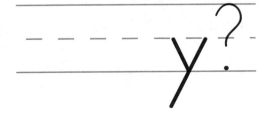

NAME ____________________

Lesson 24 Words with **wh** and **sh**

Fun with Words

Finish the spelling words to solve the puzzle.

Words Across the Curriculum 

Say each science word. Trace each word. Then, write each word.

shell shark whale

Write each science word next to the picture it names.

Lesson 24 Words with **wh** and **sh**

Words in Writing

Write about a trip you would like to make on a ship. Use at least three words from the box.

when	show	what	ship	which	shut	whale	shark	shell

_____

_ _

_____

_ _

_____

_ _

_____

which	ship	shut	when	shell

Dictionary Practice

Say the words in the box. Write them where they belong.

Short e Sound	**Short i Sound**	**Short u Sound**
_____	_____	_____
_ _ _ _ _ _ _	_ _ _ _ _ _ _	_ _ _ _ _ _ _
_____	_____	_____
_ _ _ _ _ _ _	_ _ _ _ _ _ _	_ _ _ _ _ _ _

Review Lessons 21–24

clap	fly	still	then	check	what
flat	clip	snail	this	that	ship
clam	step	stop	chop	when	which
flip	snap	snug	them	show	shut

Write the spelling word that names each picture.

_____

_____

_____

_____

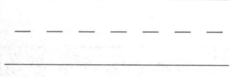
_____

Write the spelling word that rhymes with each word.

_____   _____   _____

row _____   hill _____   rug _____

_____   _____

deck _____   kiss _____

Review Lessons 21–24

Write the spelling word that fits in each sentence.

_____

– – – – – – – – –

1. _____ time is it?

_____

– – – – – – – – –

2. My bike has a _____ tire.

_____

– – – – – – – – –

3. The bus will _____ soon.

_____

– – – – – – – – –

4. _____ can we have a snack?

_____

– – – – – – – – –

5. Please _____ the door.

_____

– – – – – – – – –

6. Let's eat lunch, and _____ we can play.

_____

– – – – – – – – –

7. My dad will _____ some wood.

Lesson 25 Words with the Long **a** Sound

Spelling Words

Say each word. Listen for the long **a** sound. Trace each word. Write the word.

Spelling Tip

These letter patterns can make the long **a** sound: **a-consonant-e** and **ay**.

make

name

day

gave

way

ate

Lesson 25 Words with the Long **a** Sound

Words in Context

Write the missing spelling words.

_____   _____

- - - - - - -   - - - - - - -

When I get up every _____, I _____

_____

- - - - - -

my bed the _____ my mom showed me to do it.

_____

- - - - - - -

Then, I have breakfast. Today, I _____ eggs and

_____

- - - - - -

ham. I _____ my dog a bite

_____

- - - - - - - -

of ham. Her _____ is Kate.

Word Building

Write **a** and **e** or **ay** to make a
word that names each picture.

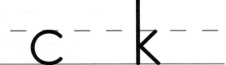

c ___ k

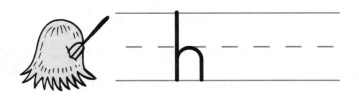

___ h ___

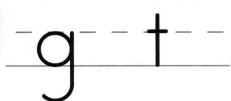

g ___ t

Lesson 25 Words with the Long a Sound

Fun with Words

Use the letters on the blocks
to write the spelling words.

_____ _____ _____

– –

_____ _____ _____

_____ _____ _____

– –

_____ _____ _____

Words Across the Curriculum

Say each art word. Trace each word. Then, write each word.

clay   same   shape

Write the missing art words.

_____   _____

– – – – – – – – –   – – – – – – – – –

You can roll _____ into the _____

of a ball.   _____

                                  – – – – – – – –

You can make another one that is the _____ size.

Lesson 25 Words with the Long **a** Sound

Words in Writing

Write about something you like to make.
Use at least three words from the box.

make	day	way	clay	same
name	gave	ate	shape	

_____

- -

_____

_____

- -

_____

_____

- -

_____

Dictionary Practice

Write the spelling words in ABC order.

make	day	way
name	gave	ate

1. _____

2. _____

3. _____

4. _____

5. _____

6. _____

Lesson 26 Words with the Long i Sound

Spelling Words

Say each word. Listen for the long **i** sound. Trace each word. Write the word.

| Spelling Tip | These letter patterns can make the long **i** sound: **i-consonant-e** and **y**. |

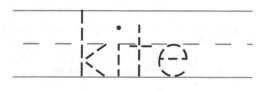

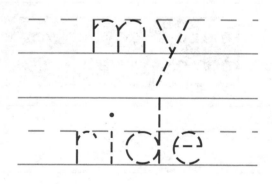

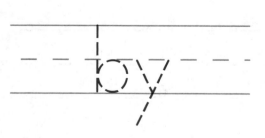

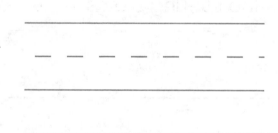

Lesson 26 Words with the Long **i** Sound

Words in Context
Write the missing spelling words.

_____   _____

— — — — — —   — — — — —

Mike is _____ best friend. We _____

_____   _____

— — — — — —   — — — — — —

to _____ our bikes. One _____,

_____

— — — — — —

we rode _____ the park. We

_____

— — — — — —

saw a boy flying a _____.

Word Building
Write **i** and **e** or **y** to make a word
that names each picture.

d __ m

v __ n

fr __

Lesson 26 Words with the Long **i** Sound

Fun with Words

Unscramble the letters to write the spelling words.

ym _____   erid _____   tiek _____

yb _____   klie _____   meti _____

Words Across the Curriculum

Say each science word. Trace each word. Then, write each word.

ice   sky   size

Write each science word
next to the picture it names.

_____

_____

Lesson 26 Words with the Long **i** Sound

Words in Writing

Write about a shopping trip. Use
at least two words from the box.

like	kite	ride	ice	size
time	my	by	sky	

_____

- -

_____

- -

_____

Misspelled Words

Circle the four misspelled words. Then, write the words correctly on
the lines below.

   The last tyme I went for a drive with mi mom, I did not lik it. We got a
flat tire on one side of the car. I had to wait bie the car while she fixed it.

_____   _____

- - - - - - - - - -   - - - - - - - - - -

_____   _____

- - - - - - - - - -   - - - - - - - - - -

_____   _____

Lesson 27 Words with the Long o Sound

Spelling Words

Say each word. Listen for the long **o** sound. Trace each word. Write the word.

Spelling Tip These letter patterns can make the long **o** sound: **o-consonant-e**, and **o**.

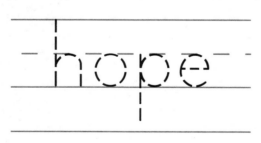

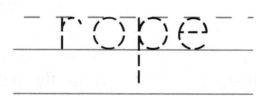

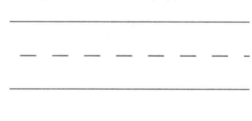

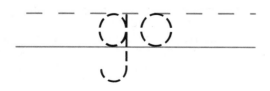

Lesson 27 Words with the Long **o** Sound

Words in Context

Write the missing spelling words.

_____

My friend wrote me a _____ today. She

_____   _____

wants me to _____ to her _____

_____

after school. We can jump _____ and play games. I

_____   _____

_____ my mom won't say _____!

Word Building

Write **o** and **e** to make a word
that names each picture.

st__ __ v__

p__ __ l

r__ __ b

Lesson 27 Words with the Long o Sound

Fun with Words

Circle the hidden spelling word on each line. Then, write the word.

o r p r o p e r p _____

o g n n o h s e _____

s e h t h o m e _____

p h o p e m e _____

Words Across the Curriculum

Say each science word. Trace each word. Then, write each word.

bone   stone   globe

Write each science word
next to the picture it names.

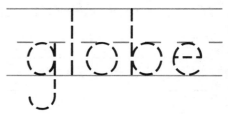

Lesson 27 Words with the Long o Sound

Words in Writing

Think about a place that you would like to
visit. Write about why you want to go there.
Use at least three words from the box.

| no | home | rope | note | hope | go | bone | stone | globe |

_____

_ _ _ _ _ _ _ _ _ _ _ _ _ _ _ _ _ _ _ _

_____

_ _ _ _ _ _ _ _ _ _ _ _ _ _ _ _ _ _ _ _

_____

_ _ _ _ _ _ _ _ _ _ _ _ _ _ _ _ _ _ _ _

_____

Dictionary Practice

Words that name people, places, and things are **nouns**. Circle the
noun in each sentence.

My home is snug.   That bone is old.

I will go soon.   Please don't step on the stone!

A globe is round.   Where is the rope?

Lesson 28 Words with the Long **e** Sound

Spelling Words

Say each word. Listen for the long **e** sound. Trace each word. Write the word.

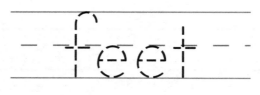

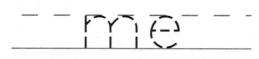

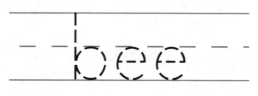

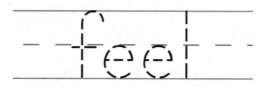

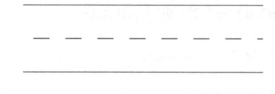

Lesson 28 Words with the Long **e** Sound

Words in Context
Write the missing spelling words.

_____

– – – – – – – – – – – –

My friend Lee is walking with _____.

_____   _____

– – – – – – – – –   – – – – – – – – – –

_____ doesn't _____ what is

_____   _____

– – – – – – – – –   – – – – – – – – –

near his _____. It is a _____! If it

_____

– – – – – – – – – –

stings him, it will not _____ good.

Word Building
Write **ee** to make a word that
names each picture.

tr __ __

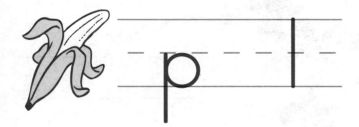

p __ __ l

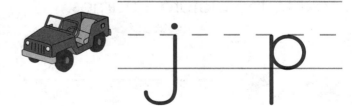

j __ __ p

Lesson 28 Words with the Long **e** Sound

Fun with Words

Use the letters in the leaves
to make the spelling words.

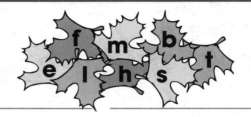

_____ _____

_ _ _ _ _ _ _ _ _   _ _ _ _ _ _ _ _ _ _ _ _ _ _ _

_____ _____

_____ _____

_____ _____

Words Across the Curriculum

Say each science word. Trace each word. Then, write each word.

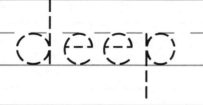 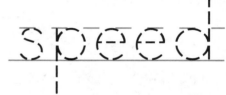

seed   deep   speed

_ _ _ _ _ _ _   _ _ _ _ _ _ _   _ _ _ _ _ _ _

Write each science word
next to the picture it names.

_ _ _ _ _ _ _ _ _ _ _ _ _

_ _ _ _ _ _ _ _ _ _ _ _ _

_ _ _ _ _ _ _ _ _ _ _ _ _

_ _ _ _ _ _ _ _ _ _ _ _ _

Lesson 28 Words with the Long e Sound

Words in Writing

Write about something you like to do outside. Use at least two words from the box.

| he | see | feet | me | bee | feel | speed | deep | seed |

_____

-- -- -- -- -- -- -- -- -- -- -- -- -- -- -- --

_____

-- -- -- -- -- -- -- -- -- -- -- -- -- -- -- --

_____

Misspelled Words

Circle the misspelled word in each row. Then, write the word correctly.

_____

-- -- -- -- -- -- --

me   bee   se   _____

-- -- -- -- -- -- --

feet   dep   he   _____

-- -- -- -- -- --

speed   weed   fel   _____

Review Lessons 25–28

make	way	kite	no	hope	feet
name	ate	my	home	go	me
day	like	ride	rope	he	bee
gave	time	by	note	see	feel

Write the spelling word that names each picture.

 _____

 _____

 _____

 _____

Write the two spelling words that rhyme with each word.

why   hay   so

_____   _____   _____

_____   _____   _____

_____   _____   _____

_____   _____   _____

Review Lessons 25–28

Read each word. Write the two spelling words that have the same beginning sound.

_____   _____

- - - - - - - - -   - - - - - - - - -

rip _____   _____

_____   _____

- - - - - - - - -   - - - - - - - - -

mop _____   _____

LESSONS 25-28 REVIEW

Write the spelling word that belongs in each sentence.

_____

- - - - - - - -

We _____ ham and eggs.

_____

- - - - - - - -

I _____ my mom a kiss.

_____

- - - - - - - - -

Do you _____ to ride a bike?

_____

- - - - - - - - -

What is your dog's _____?

Lesson 29 Words You Use Often

Spelling Words
Say each word. Trace each word. Then, write the word.

| Spelling Tip | Some words aren't spelled the way they sound. You have to remember how to spell them. |

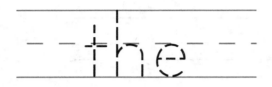

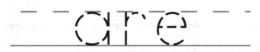

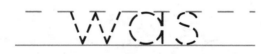

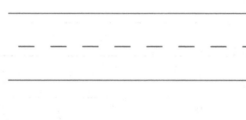

Lesson 29 Words You Use Often

Words in Context
Write the missing spelling words.

_____

I _____ late for

_____

_____ party!

" _____   _____

_____ must hurry," _____ my mom.

_____   _____

Your friends _____ waiting _____ you.

Word Building
A **contraction** is two words joined into one shorter word. Look at the contractions in the box. Then, write the contractions where they belong.

> are not = aren't
> was not = wasn't
> you are = you're

was not   you are   are not

_____   _____   _____

_____   _____   _____

Lesson 29 Words You Use Often

Fun with Words

Match the beginning letter of each spelling word with the rest of its letters.

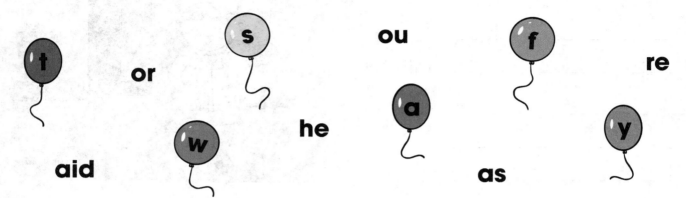

or

aid

he

ou

as

re

Words Across the Curriculum

Say each math word. Trace each word. Then, write each word.

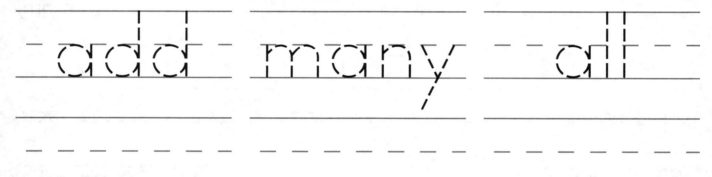

Write each math word below its meaning.

every one	a lot	sum

Lesson 29 Words You Use Often

Words in Writing

Write about a time when you have to count things. Use at least three words from the box.

the	for	said	add	all
are	was	said	you	many

_____

- -

_____

_____

_____

- -

_____

Dictionary Practice

Write the spelling words in ABC order.

the	for	said
are	was	you

1. _____   3. _____   5. _____

2. _____   4. _____   6. _____

Lesson 30 More Words You Use Often

Spelling Words
Say each word. Trace each word. Then, write the word.

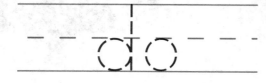

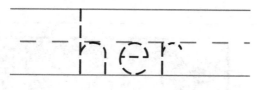

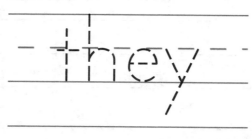

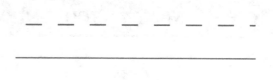

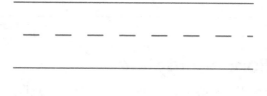
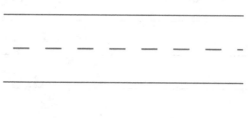

Lesson 30 More Words You Use Often

Words in Context

Write the missing spelling words.

_____   _____

— — — — — — — - -   — — — — — — — - -

I _____ two friends who _____

                          _____

                          — — — — — — — - -

to play. I'll ask Mom if I need to _____ some work

        _____   _____

        — — — — — — — - -   — — — — — — — - -

first. Then, I'll ask _____ if _____

        _____

        — — — — — — — -

can _____ over.

Word Building

Add **s** to tell what a boy is doing.

I make. He make_____.

I like. He like_____.

I ride. He rides.

I want. He want_____.

I see. He see_____.

Lesson 30 More Words You Use Often

Fun with Words
Circle the hidden
spelling words.

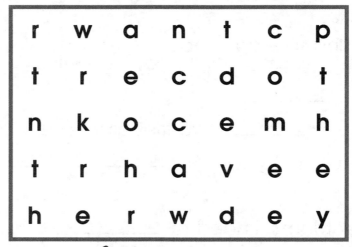

r	w	a	n	t	c	p
t	r	e	c	d	o	t
n	k	o	c	e	m	h
t	r	h	a	v	e	e
h	e	r	w	d	e	y

Words Across the Curriculum

Say each math word. Trace each word. Then, write each word.

and   some   here

Write the missing letter to
complete each math word.

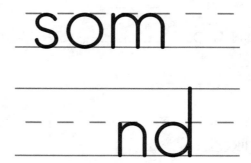

som

h__re   __nd

Lesson 30 More Words You Use Often

Words in Writing

Do you like people to visit you at home?
Write about your favorite visitors. Use at
least three words from the box.

do	come	they	and	here
have	her	want	some	

_____

- - - - - - - - - - - - - - - - - - - -

_____

- - - - - - - - - - - - - - - - - - - -

_____

- - - - - - - - - - - - - - - - - - - -

_____

Misspelled Words

Circle the word in each pair that is not spelled correctly.

they	thay		cume	come
dou	do		hur	her
have	hav		want	wonte

Lesson 31 Color Words

Spelling Words
Say each word.
Trace each word.
Then, write the word.

| Spelling Tip | Some words are spelled the way they sound. Some words aren't. You have to remember how to spell words that aren't spelled the way they sound. |

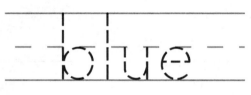

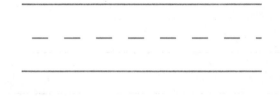

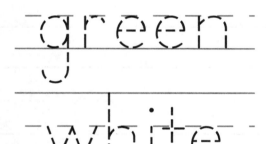

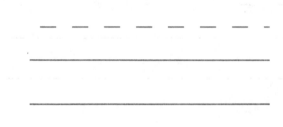

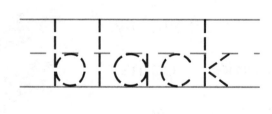

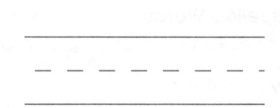

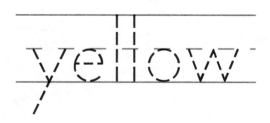

Lesson 31 Color Words

Words in Context

Write the missing spelling words.

_____

- - - - - - - - - - - -

The sky is _____.

_____   _____

- - - - - - - - - -   - - - - - - - - - -

Grass is _____.   The sun is _____.

_____

- - - - - - - - - -

An apple is _____.

_____   _____

- - - - - - - - - -   - - - - - - - - - -

A zebra is _____ and _____.

Word Building

Write **ay**, **i**, or **o** to make
a color word.

p nk

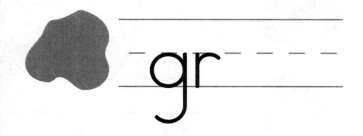

gr

g ld

Lesson 31 Color Words

Fun with Words

Write each color word where it belongs.

Words Across the Curriculum

Say each art word. Trace each word. Then, write each word.

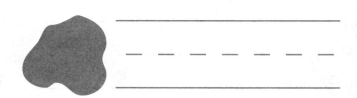

Write each art word next
to the picture it names.

Lesson 31 Color Words

Words in Writing

What do different colors make you think of? Write about the colors of some things. Use at least three words from the box.

red	green	black	purple	brown
blue	white	yellow	orange	

_____

- -

_____

- -

_____

- -

_____

- -

_____

- -

Dictionary Practice

Write the spelling word that has each vowel sound listed below.

Short a Sound   **Long e Sound**   **Long i Sound**

_____   _____   _____

- - - - - - - -   - - - - - - - -   - - - - - - - -

_____   _____   _____

Review Lessons 29–31

the	was	do	her	red	white
are	said	have	they	blue	black
for	you	come	want	green	yellow

Write the two spelling words that have the same beginning sound as each picture.

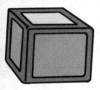

_____   _____

_____   _____

_____   _____

_____   _____

Write the color word that belongs with each color below.

_____   _____

_____    _____

_____

Review Lessons 29–31

Write **s** to make a spelling word.

wa ___ ___ he ___ aid

Write the missing spelling words.

_____

I will make a cake _____ my mom.

_____

Where _____ you going?

_____

What do you _____ to do?

_____

Let's go to _____ zoo.

_____

Do you _____ a bike?

A

add *v.* To find the sum; to put together with another.

all *adj.* Everything.

and *conj.* Together with.

are *v.* Live or exist; to be.

ate *v.* Past tense of *eat*. Took in food.

B

bag *n.* A sack used for holding, storing, or carrying.

bed *n.* A place for sleeping.

bee *n.* A flying insect with a hairy body.

big *adj.* Large.

black *adj.* The darkest color.

blue *adj.* The color of a clear sky.

bone *n.* The hard part of a skeleton.

box *n.* A cube used to keep things in.

brown *adj.* The color of a tree trunk and soil.

but *conj.* In contrast; even so.

by *prep.* Close to; past.

C

can *n.* A metal cylinder to keep food in. *v.* To be able to.

cat *n.* A small, furry animal kept as a pet and to catch mice and rats.

chart *n.* A map, graph, or table.

check *v.* To look at for correctness.

chop *v.* To cut into small pieces.

clam *n.* An animal with a soft body and hard shell that opens and closes.

clap *v.* To make a sound by hitting the hands together.

clay *n.* Wet soil that hardens when it dries, used to make pottery, bricks, and tiles.

clip *n.* A small tool that holds things together.

club *n.* A group of people who meet together for a reason.

come *v.* To arrive.

cup *n.* A small, open container used for drinking.

D

dad *n.* A father.

day *n.* Twenty-four hours.

deep *adj.* Far below a surface.

did *v.* Past tense of *do*.

dig *v.* To make a hole in the ground.

do *v.* To carry out or perform; to finish.

E

egg *n.* The hard-shelled, oval body produced by birds and other animals.

F

feel *v.* To observe through touching; to be aware of.

feet *n.* The plural of *foot.* The end part of the leg, used for walking.

fin *n.* A thin, movable part of the body of a fish.

fit *v.* To make the right size and shape.

flag *n.* A piece of cloth with colors and designs to represent a country, state, or club.

flat *adj.* Stretched out; having no air inside.

flip *n.* A quick turning through the air. *v.* To turn or throw over suddenly.

fly *n.* A winged insect. *v.* To travel by air.

fun *n.* Something that entertains.

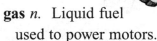

G

gas *n.* Liquid fuel used to power motors.

gave *v.* Past tense of *give.* Made a gift of; handed over.

get *v.* To earn, gain, or come into possession of.

globe *n.* A model of Earth.

go *v.* To move away from.

got *v.* Past tense of *get.* To receive something.

green *adj.* The color of grass.

H

hand *n.* The part of the arm below the wrist, consisting of the palm, four fingers, and a thumb.

have *v.* To possess.

he *pron.* A male human being.

hen *n.* An adult female chicken.

her *pron.* A female human being.

here *adv.* To, at, or in this place.

hide *v.* To keep out of sight; to keep secret.

hill *n.* A rounded, raised part of land.

him *pron.* A male human being.

home *n.* The place where one lives.

hope *v.* To want or wish for something.

hug *v.* To put one's arms around someone or something.

I

ice *n.* Frozen water.

is *v.* Third person, singular, present tense of the verb *to be.*

J

job *n.* Work.

L

like *adj.* The same or similar. *v.* To enjoy.
lock *n.* A device used to close away or secure. *v.* To close with a lock.

M

make *v.* To create.
man·y *adj.* A large number.
math *n.* A subject that uses numbers.
me *pron.* The person I am.
mom *n.* A mother.
much *adj.* A great amount.
mud *n.* A mixture of water and soil.
my *adj.* Relating to me.

N

name *n.* A word that tells who or what someone or something is.
no *adv.* Not at all.
not *adv.* In no way.
note *n.* A short letter or message.
nut *n.* A seed or fruit from a plant.

O

or·ange *adj.* Yellowish red. *n.* A citrus fruit round and orange in color.

P

pet *n.* An animal, bird, or fish that a person keeps for companionship.
pig *n.* A fat animal with short legs and a snout.
pot *n.* A rounded, deep container used for cooking.
pur·ple *adj.* A color also called *violet*.

R

ran *v.* Past tense of *run*. Moved quickly with the legs.
red *n.* The color of a stop sign.
ride *v.* To sit on and be carried, as on a bike or an animal.
rope *n.* A heavy cord made of twisted fiber.
run *v.* To move quickly with the legs.

S

said *v.* Past tense of *say*. Spoke.

same *adj.* Alike or identical.

sand *n.* Fine grains of rock found in deserts and on beaches.

sat *v.* Past tense of *sit*. To rest on a seat.

see *v.* To observe with the eyes.

seed *n.* A small part of a plant that grows into a new plant.

shape *n.* An outline or figure.

shark *n.* A large, dangerous fish.

shell *n.* The hard, outer covering of certain animals.

ship *n.* A large boat for deep-water travel.

shop *n.* A small store. *v.* To look for things to buy.

show *v.* To point out.

shut *v.* To close.

size *n.* The amount of space that something takes up.

sky *n.* The space above the Earth.

snail *n.* An animal that lives in a spiral shell.

snake *n.* A reptile with no legs.

snap *v.* To break suddenly with a sharp, quick sound. To move the fingers together to make a sound.

snow *n.* Water that forms crystals in cold air and falls to the ground in white flakes. *v.* To fall as snow.

snug *adj.* Warm, pleasant, comfortable.

some *adj.* Being an unknown number or amount.

speed *n.* Rate of action or movement.

star *n.* A body of bright light that can be seen in the night sky.

stem *n.* The main stalk of a plant.

step *n.* A single movement in walking. *v.* To move one foot forward or backward.

still *adj.* Calm.

stone *n.* A rock.

stop *v.* To end a movement.

sun *n.* The star around which Earth and other planets revolve.

T

that *adj.* The person or thing present or being mentioned.

the *art.* Used before naming a person, place, or thing.

then *adv.* At that time.

they *pron.* The two or more beings or things just mentioned.

this *pron.* The person or thing that is near, present, or just mentioned.

time *n.* A period measured by clocks, watches, and calendars.

top *n.* The highest part of anything.

tub *n.* A large container used for washing.

W

want *v.* To wish for.

was *v.* Past tense of *be*. Existed or happened.

way *n.* A manner of doing something.

web *n.* A network of threads made by a spider.

wet *adj.* Covered with water or other liquid.

whale *n.* A very large mammal resembling a fish that lives in salt water.

what *pron.* Which one?

when *adv.* At what time?

which *pron.* What one or ones?

white *adj.* The color opposite of black.

Y

yel·low *adj.* The color of a lemon.

yes *adv.* An expression of agreement.

you *pron.* The person or persons being spoken to.

Parts of Speech

adj. = *adjective*

adv. = *adverb*

art. = *article*

conj. = *conjunction*

n. = *noun*

prep. = *preposition*

pron. = *pronoun*

v. = *verb*

Answer Key

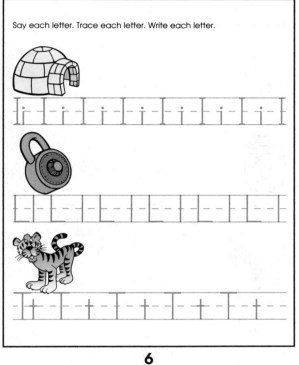

Say each letter. Trace each letter. Write each letter.

Say each letter. Trace each letter. Write each letter.

6

7

Say each letter. Trace each letter. Write each letter.

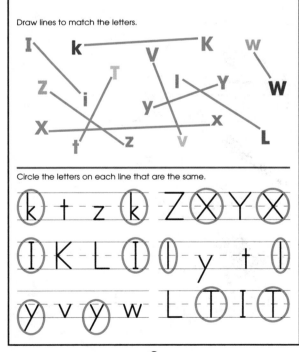

Draw lines to match the letters.

Circle the letters on each line that are the same.

8

9

Say each letter. Trace each letter. Write each letter.

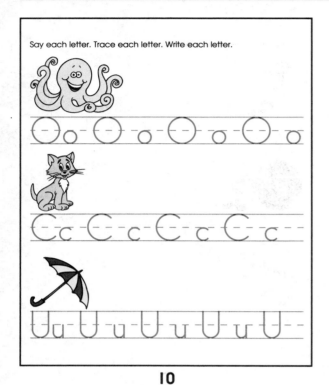

Say each letter. Trace each letter. Write each letter.

10

11

Say each letter. Trace each letter. Write each letter.

Find the letters **O, C, U, S, J, G, P, B**, and **D**. Circle each letter.

12

13

Answer Key

Say each letter. Trace each letter. Write each letter.

Hh Hh Hh Hh H

Mm M m M m M

Nn Nn Nn Nn N

14

Say each letter. Trace each letter. Write each letter.

Aa Aa Aa Aa

Ee Ee Ee Ee

Qq Qq Qq Qq

15

Say each letter. Trace each letter. Write each letter.

Rr Rr Rr Rr R

Ff Ff Ff Ff f

Trace each word. Write each word.

fan fan ham ham

16

Find the letters **h**, **m**, **n**, **a**, **e**, **q**, **r**, and **f**. Circle each letter.

monkeys

squirrel

giraffe

elephants

deer

foxes

17

Answer Key

Name each picture. Circle the letter for the beginning sounds.

t m s j c

t j (c)	s t (m)	(t) j s
c m (j)	m t (s)	c j (m)
t (c) s	(s) c m	c m (t)

18

Name the pictures. Circle the pictures in each row with the same beginning sound. Write the letter for the beginning sound.

c

j

t

s

m

19

Name each picture. Write the letter for the beginning sound.

t m s j c

c   t

r   j

s   c

t   m

m   s

20

Name each picture. Write the letter for the beginning sound. Circle the correct word.

t	mop / (top)
j	(jar) / car
m	(map) / cap
s	(six) / mix
c	mat / (cat)

21

Spectrum Spelling
Grade 1
152

Answer Key

Answer Key

Name each picture. Circle the letter for the beginning sound.

d f g n w

d (g) w	(w) f n	(n) g d
d g (f)	g (d) n	(n) w d
g n (d)	d (f) g	(w) n g

22

Name the pictures. Circle the pictures in each row with the same beginning sound. Write the letter for the beginning sound.

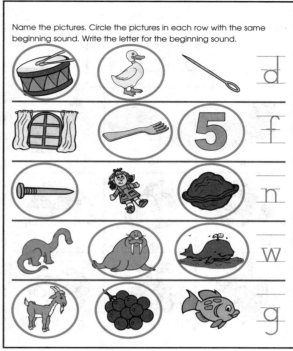

d

f

n

w

g

23

Name each picture. Write the letter for the beginning sound.

d f g n w

g   w

w   d

d   f

n   g

f   n

24

Name each picture. Write the letter for the beginning sound. Then, circle the correct word. Write the correct word.

🐕	d	fog (dog)	dog
🧺	n	wet (net)	net
🚪	g	date (gate)	gate
👱	w	(wig) dig	wig
🐟	f	wish (fish)	fish

25

Spectrum Spelling
Grade 1

Answer Key

Answer Key

26

Name the pictures. Circle the pictures in each row with the same beginning sound. Write the letter for the beginning sound.

r

b

p

h

b

27

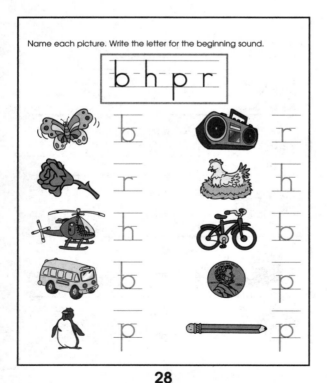

28

Name each picture. Write the letter for the beginning sound. Circle the correct word.

	p	big / **pig**
	h	**hat** / bat
	h	**hen** / pen
	r	bug / **rug**
	b	hall / **ball**

29

Answer Key

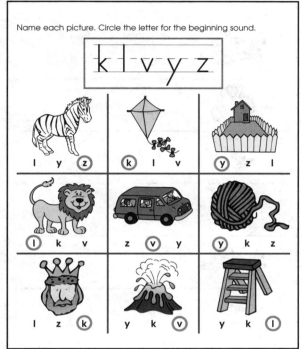

Name each picture. Circle the letter for the beginning sound.

k l v y z

Name the pictures. Circle the pictures in each row with the same beginning sound. Write the letter for the beginning sound.

k
t
z
v
y

30

31

Name each picture. Write the letter for the beginning sound.

k l v y z

v
k
l
z
y

v
k
z
y
l

32

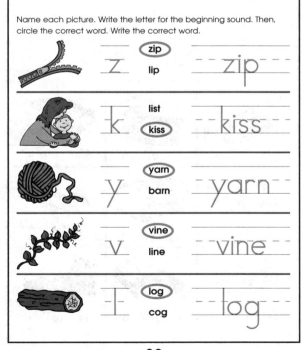

Name each picture. Write the letter for the beginning sound. Then, circle the correct word. Write the correct word.

z — (zip) / lip — zip

k — list / (kiss) — kiss

y — (yarn) / barn — yarn

v — (vine) / line — vine

l — (log) / cog — log

33

Answer Key

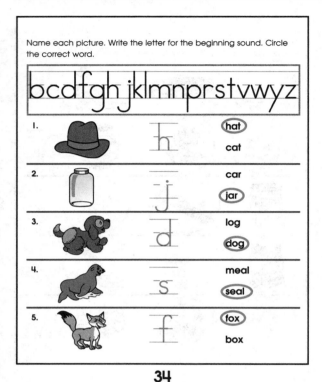

Name each picture. Write the letter for the beginning sound. Circle the correct word.

b c d f g h j k l m n p r s t v w y z

1. h — (hat) / cat
2. j — car / (jar)
3. d — log / (dog)
4. s — meal / (seal)
5. f — (fox) / box

34

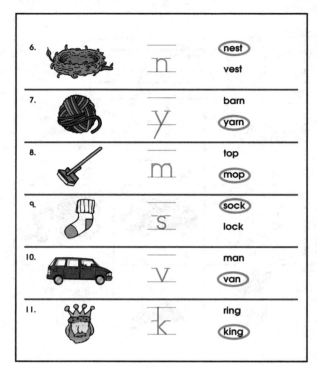

6. n — (nest) / vest
7. y — barn / (yarn)
8. m — top / (mop)
9. s — (sock) / lock
10. v — man / (van)
11. k — ring / (king)

35

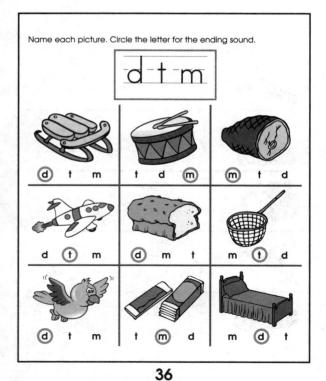

Name each picture. Circle the letter for the ending sound.

d t m

(d) t m   t d (m)   (m) t d
d (t) m   (d) m t   m (t) d
(d) t m   t (m) d   m (d) t

36

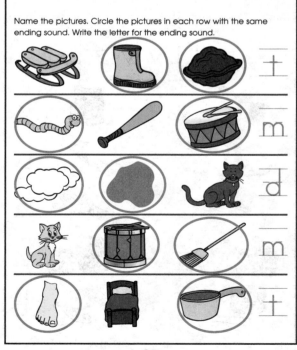

Name the pictures. Circle the pictures in each row with the same ending sound. Write the letter for the ending sound.

t
m
d
m
t

37

Answer Key

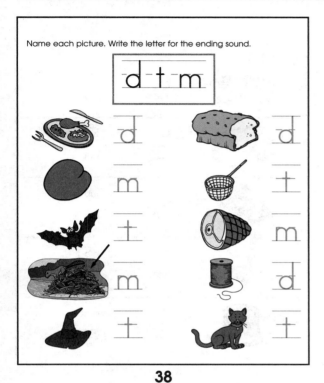

38

Name each picture. Write the letter for the ending sound.

d t m

d   d
m   t
t   m
m   d
t   t

39

Name each picture. Write the letter for the ending sound. Circle the correct word.

t   ham
         (hat)

m   (ram)
         rat

t   (pot)
         pod

d   bad
         (bed)

d   (food)
         foot

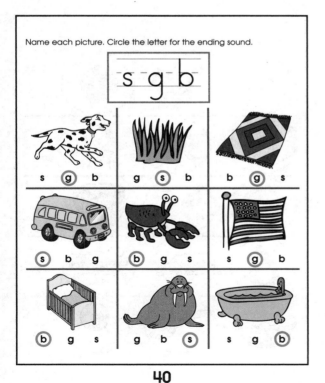

40

Name each picture. Circle the letter for the ending sound.

s g b

s (g) b   g (s) b   b (g) s
(s) b g   (b) g s   s (g) b
(b) g s   g b (s)   s g (b)

41

Name the pictures. Circle the pictures in each row with the same ending sound. Write the letter for the ending sound.

g
s
g
b
g

Answer Key

Name each picture. Write the letter for the ending sound.

```
 s g b
```

g   s
s   b
g   b
b   s
g   g

42

Name each picture. Write the letter for the ending sound. Circle the correct word.

b   (tub)
     tug

s   (bus)
     bug

g   rub
     (rug)

b   (bib)
     big

s   grab
     (gas)

43

Name each picture. Circle the letter for the ending sound.

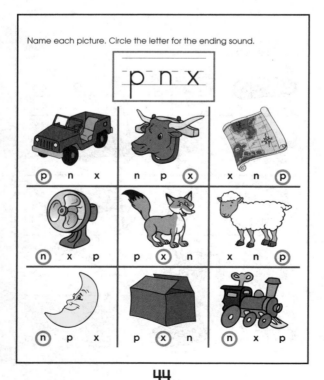

```
 p n x
```

(p) n x   n p (x)   x n (p)

(n) x p   p (x) n   x n (p)

(n) p x   p (x) n   (n) x p

44

Name the pictures. Circle the pictures in each row with the same ending sound. Write the letter for the ending sound.

p
x
n
x
n

45

Spectrum Spelling
Grade 1

Answer Key

Answer Key

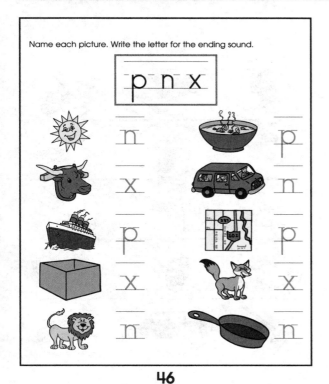

Name each picture. Write the letter for the ending sound.

```
p n x
```

☀ n	🍲 p
🐂 x	🚐 n
🚢 p	🗺 p
📦 x	🦊 x
🦁 n	🍳 n

46

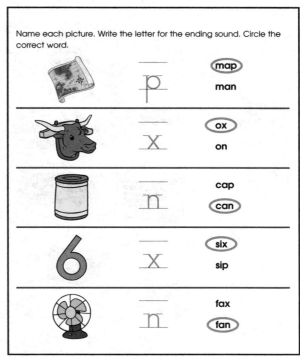

Name each picture. Write the letter for the ending sound. Circle the correct word.

🗺	p	(map) / man
🐂	x	(ox) / on
🥫	n	cap / (can)
6	x	(six) / sip
🌀	n	fax / (fan)

47

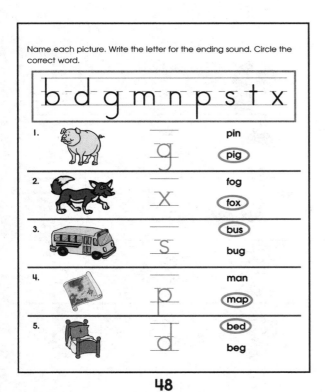

Name each picture. Write the letter for the ending sound. Circle the correct word.

```
b d g m n p s t x
```

1. 🐷   g   pin / (pig)
2. 🦊   x   fog / (fox)
3. 🚌   s   (bus) / bug
4. 🗺   p   man / (map)
5. 🛏   d   (bed) / beg

48

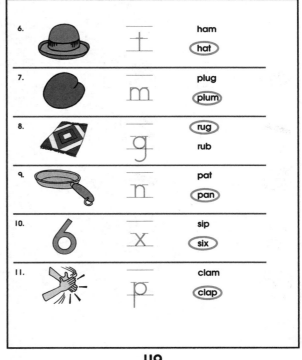

6. 🎩   t   ham / (hat)
7. 🫐   m   plug / (plum)
8. 🔷   g   (rug) / rub
9. 🍳   n   pat / (pan)
10. 6   x   sip / (six)
11. 👏   p   clam / (clap)

49

Spectrum Spelling
Grade 1

Answer Key

Say **hat**.

Name each picture. Listen for the short **a** sound as in **hat**. Circle the pictures with the short **a** sound.

50

Name each picture. Listen for the short **a** sound. Circle the pictures with the short **a** sound.

51

Name each picture. Listen for the short **a** sound. Write **a** on the line if you hear the short **a** sound.

hat	bag
p n	map
flag	van
cat	p g
c p	stamp

52

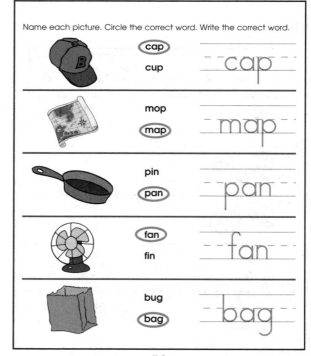

Name each picture. Circle the correct word. Write the correct word.

(cap) cup		cap
mop (map)		map
pin (pan)		pan
(fan) fin		fan
bug (bag)		bag

53

Answer Key

Say **pin**.

Name each picture. Listen for the short **i** sound as in **pin**. Circle the pictures with the short **i** sound.

54

Name the pictures. Listen for the short **i** sound. Circle the pictures in each row with the short **i** sound.

55

Name each picture. Listen for the short **i** sound. Write **i** on the line if you hear the short **i** sound.

i

🐟 f i sh   🦆 b i b

🦞 cr i b   🛷 s l d

🧷 p i n   6 s i x

🥣 d i sh   🚢 sh i p

🦊 f x   🫓 l i d

56

Name each picture. Circle the correct word. Write the correct word.

	hall / (hill)	hill
	(pin) / pan	pin
	(crib) / crab	crib
	(wig) / wag	wig
	clap / (clip)	clip

57

Answer Key

Say **top**.

Name each picture. Listen for the short **o** sound as in **top**. Circle the pictures with the short **o** sound.

58

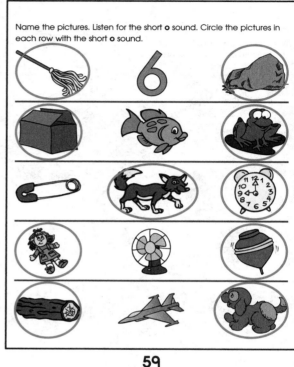

Name the pictures. Listen for the short **o** sound. Circle the pictures in each row with the short **o** sound.

59

Name each picture. Listen for the short **o** sound. Write **o** on the line if you hear the short **o** sound.

m _ p   c _ p
t o ck   f o x
h _ t   s o ck
d o ll   t _ b
p o t   l o g

60

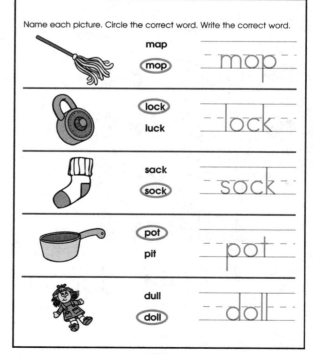

Name each picture. Circle the correct word. Write the correct word.

map
(mop)   mop

(lock)
luck   lock

sack
(sock)   sock

(pot)
pit   pot

dull
(doll)   doll

61

Answer Key

Say **cup**.

Name each picture. Listen for the short **u** sound as in **cup**. Circle the pictures with the short **u** sound.

62

Name the pictures. Listen for the short **u** sound. Circle the pictures in each row with the short **u** sound.

63

Name each picture. Listen for the short **u** sound. Write **u** on the line if you hear the short **u** sound.

$\underline{u}$

duck	nut
sun	cup
b_ll	f_sh
fr_g	bus
tub	bug

64

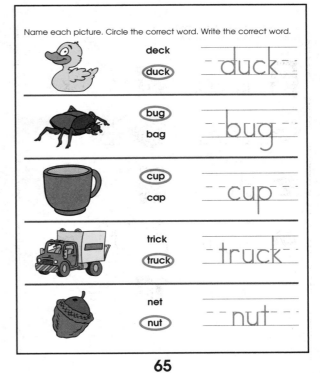

Name each picture. Circle the correct word. Write the correct word.

deck / (duck)	duck
(bug) / bag	bug
(cup) / cap	cup
trick / (truck)	truck
net / (nut)	nut

65

Answer Key

66

67

68

69

Answer Key

Name the first picture in each row. Name the other pictures. Circle the picture with the same middle sound as the first picture. Write the letter of the middle sound.

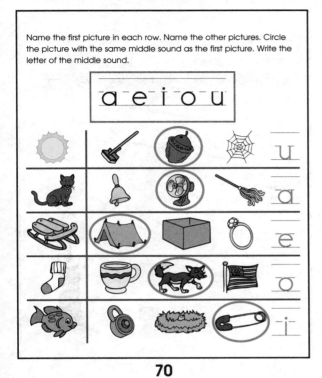

| a | e | i | o | u |

u
a
e
o
i

70

Name each picture. Write the letter for the middle sound. Circle the word that names the picture.

u   deck / (duck) / dock

a   bell / (bull) / (ball)

e   (net) / nut / not

o   sack / (sock) / sick

i   (hill) / hall / hull

71

Spelling Words
Say each word. Listen for the short **a** sound. Trace each word. Write the word.

ran   ran

can   can

cat   cat

sat   sat

dad   dad

bag   bag

72

Words in Context
Write the missing spelling words.

My ___cat___ jumped out of the tree.

It ___ran___ to the van with me.

We ___sat___ in the back of the van.

My ___dad___ had my soccer ___bag___.

We will go as soon as we ___can___.

Word Building
Write the letter to make words with the short **a** sound.

fan / bat / man

73

Spectrum Spelling
Grade 1

Answer Key

165

Answer Key

Fun with Words
Find the spelling words.
Look across and down.
Circle each one.

Words Across the Curriculum
Say each science word. Trace each word. Then, write each word.

gas hand sand

gas hand sand

Write each science word
next to the picture it names.

sand

hand gas

74

Words in Writing
Write about a time you went to a park.
Use at least two words from the box.

| ran | can | cat | sat | dad | bag | gas | sand | hand |

Answers will vary.

Dictionary Practice
Write the word in each row that comes first in ABC order.

cat   sat   bag   bag

gas   can   ran   can

sand   dad   hand   dad

75

Spelling Words
Say each word. Listen for the short **i** sound. Trace each word.
Write the word.

did   did

big   big

fit   fit

pig   pig

him   him

is   is

76

Words in Context
Write the missing spelling words.

I have a pet __pig__.

He __is__ pink, and very, very __big__.

I __did__ call __him__ Tiny Tim.

But that name does not __fit__.

Word Building
Write the letter to make words with the short **i** sound.

s i t   d i sh

l i d   b i b

77

Answer Key

Fun with Words

Say each word. Write the spelling word or words that rhyme with each word.

sit _fit_   rim _him_   hid _did_

fizz _is_   jig _big_, _pig_

Words Across the Curriculum

Say each science word. Trace each word. Then, write each word.

fin   _hill_   _dig_

fin   _hill_   _dig_

Write each science word next to the picture it names.

dig

hill   _fin_

78

Words in Writing

Write about what a farm is like. Use at least two words from the box.

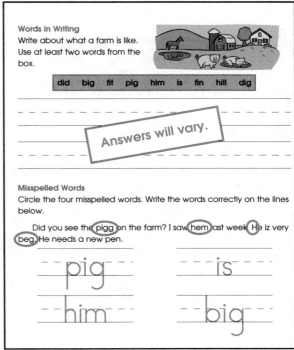

| did | big | fit | pig | him | is | fin | hill | dig |

Answers will vary.

Misspelled Words

Circle the four misspelled words. Write the words correctly on the lines below.

Did you see the (pigg) on the farm? I saw (hem) last week. He (iz) very (beg). He needs a new pen.

pig   _is_

him   _big_

79

Spelling Words

Say each word. Listen for the short **o** sound. Trace each word. Write the word.

got   _got_

box   _box_

mom   _mom_

not   _not_

top   _top_

pot   _pot_

80

Words in Context

Write the missing spelling words.

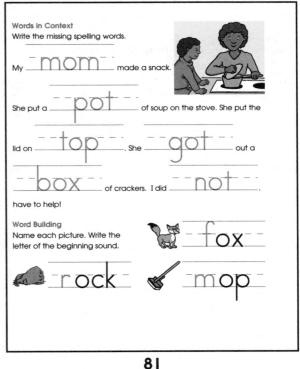

My _mom_ made a snack.

She put a _pot_ of soup on the stove. She put the

lid on _top_. She _got_ out a

box of crackers. I did _not_

have to help!

Word Building

Name each picture. Write the letter of the beginning sound.

_f_ox

_r_ock   _m_op

81

Answer Key

Page 82

Fun with Words

Look at the letters on the blocks. Use the letters to make the spelling words.

pot   not   got

top   box   mom

Words Across the Curriculum

Say each social studies word. Trace each word. Then, write each word.

shop   job   lock

shop   job   lock

Write each social studies word next to its meaning.

close lock   store shop   work job

82

Page 83

Words in Writing

Write about what your mom or dad likes to do. Use at least three words from the box.

| got | box | mom | not | top | pot | shop | job | lock |

Answers will vary.

Dictionary Practice

Write the missing letters in ABC order.

a b c d e f g h i j k l m

n o p q r s t u v w x y z

83

Page 84

Spelling Words

Say each word. Listen for the short **u** sound. Trace each word. Write the word.

run   run

hug   hug

sun   sun

but   but

fun   fun

tub   tub

84

Page 85

Words in Context

Write the missing spelling words.

Do you like to run on the beach? It's

fun ! The sand seems to hug

your feet, but they still feel

free. The sun is warm on your

body. The sea is much better than a bath in a tub

Word Building

Name each picture. Write the letter of the ending sound.

cup   rug   bus

85

Answer Key

Fun with Words

Look at each row of letters. There is a spelling word hidden in each row. Circle the word. Then, write it.

f a e (f u n) u   **fun**   u s (h u g h) b   **hug**

t s h f (b u t)   **but**   n a (s u n) u g b   **sun**

Words Across the Curriculum

Say each science word. Trace each word. Then, write each word.

nut   **cub**   **mud**

nut   **cub**   **mud**

Write each science word next to the picture it names.

nut

mud   **cub**

86

Words in Writing

Write about something you do that is fun. Use at least two words from the box.

run	sun	fun	nut	mud
hug	but	tub	cub	

Answers will vary.

Misspelled Words

Circle the four misspelled words. Then, write the sentence and spell the words correctly.

It's (fune) to (runn) in the (sen) (bot) then you need a bath.

It's fun to run in the sun, but then you need a bath.

87

Spelling Words

Say each word. Listen for the short **e** sound. Trace each word. Write the word.

get   **get**

bed   **bed**

yes   **yes**

wet   **wet**

hen   **hen**

pet   **pet**

88

Words in Context

Write the missing spelling words.

I have a funny **pet**. She sleeps on a nest instead

of a bed. Can you guess what she is? **Yes**, she's

a **hen**. She likes to **get**

wet, so she swims

in the pond.

Word Building

Name each picture. Write the letter of the beginning sound.

leg

jet   **10** **ten**

89

Spectrum Spelling
Grade 1

Answer Key

Page 90

Fun with Words
Name each picture. Write the spelling word that has the same beginning sound.

yes   bed   pet

get   hen   wet

Words Across the Curriculum
Say each science word. Trace each word. Then, write each word.

egg   stem   web

egg   stem   web

Write the science word that goes with each clue.

a spider's home   web

part of a flower   stem   found in a nest   egg

90

Page 91

Words in Writing
Write about a pet you would like to have. Use at least three words from the box.

| get | yes | hen | egg | web |
| bed | wet | pet | stem | |

Answers will vary.

Dictionary Practice
Write the spelling words in ABC order.

| get | yes | hen |
| bed | wet | pet |

1. bed   3. get   5. hen

2. pet   4. wet   6. yes

91

Page 92

ran	did	got	run	get
can	big	box	hug	bed
cat	fit	mom	sun	yes
sat	pig	not	but	wet
dad	him	top	fun	hen
bag	is	pot	tub	pet

Write the spelling word that means the opposite.

no yes   small big   dad mom

dry wet   her him

Write the spelling word that rhymes.

nut but   fox box   rub tub

men hen   lit fit

92

Page 93

Write the spelling word that goes with each pair of words.

kiss, love hug   tiger, lion cat

bottom, side top   sleep, blanket bed

cow, hen pig

Write the spelling word that fits in each sentence.

I can run fast.   The sun is shining.

I got a new toy.   The pot is on the stove.

It's fun to go to the park.

93

Spectrum Spelling
Grade 1

Answer Key

Spelling Words
Say each word. Listen to the beginning sound. Trace each word.
Write the word.

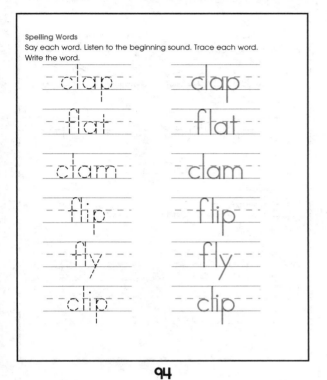

clap   clap

flat   flat

clam   clam

flip   flip

fly   fly

clip   clip

94

Words in Context
Write each spelling word next to the picture it names.

flat   clap

clam   flip

fly   clip

Word Building
Write **cl** or **fl** to make words.

flower

clock   cloud

95

Fun with Words
Find the spelling words. Look across and down. Circle each one.

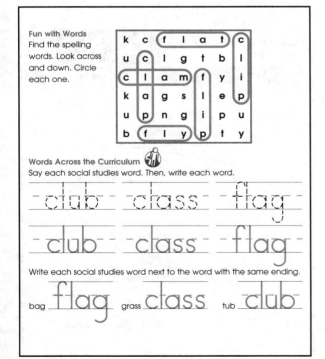

k	c	f	l	a	t	c
u	c	l	g	t	b	l
c	l	a	m	f	y	i
k	a	g	s	l	e	p
u	p	n	g	i	p	u
b	f	l	y	p	t	y

Words Across the Curriculum
Say each social studies word. Then, write each word.

club   class   flag

club   class   flag

Write each social studies word next to the word with the same ending.

bag flag   grass class   tub club

96

Words in Writing
Write two tongue-twisters. Use at least two words from the box.

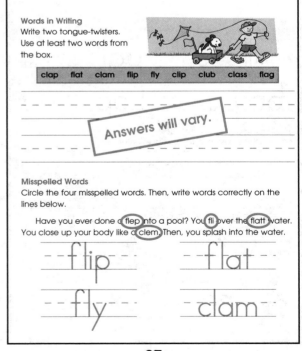

| clap | flat | clam | flip | fly | clip | club | class | flag |

Answers will vary.

Misspelled Words
Circle the four misspelled words. Then, write words correctly on the lines below.

Have you ever done a flep into a pool? You fli over the flatt water. You close up your body like a clem. Then, you splash into the water.

flip   flat

fly   clam

97

Answer Key

Spelling Words
Say each word. Listen to the beginning sound. Trace each word.
Write the word.

step   step

snap   snap

still   still

snail   snail

stop   stop

snug   snug

98

Words in Context
Write the missing spelling words.

I was warm and __snug__ in my tent. Then, I heard a twig

__snap__. I got up and took a __step__

outside. I saw a __snail__. It did not

__stop__ moving, but it __still__

didn't go very fast.

Word Building
Write **s** to the end to make words
that mean more than one. Then,
write the new words.

snap __s__ snaps

step __s__ steps   stop __s__ stops

99

Fun with Words
Write the spelling word that rhymes with each word.

hill still   pail snail

bug snug   hop stop

Words Across the Curriculum
Say each science word. Then, write each word.

star snow snake

star snow snake

Write each science word next
to the picture it names.

star

snake   snow

100

Words in Writing
Make up a story. Use at least
three words from the box.

| step | snap | still | snail | stop | snug | star | snow | snake |

Answers will vary.

Dictionary Practice
A **verb** is a word that tells what happens. Circle the verb in each
sentence.

Please (stop) that dog!   Can you (snap) your fingers?

The snail (moves) slowly.   Did you (step) on the grass?

101

Page 102

Spelling Words

Say each word. Listen to the beginning sound. Trace each word. Write the word.

then   then

this   this

chop   chop

them   them

check   check

that   that

102

Page 103

Words in Context

Write the missing spelling words.

This is how my dad makes soup. He will chop vegetables. Then, he will boil them. After an hour, my dad will check to see if his soup is done. Doesn't that sound easy?

Word Building

Add **ch** or **th** to make words that fit the meanings. Then, write the words.

talk with a friend   chat   chat

skinny   thin   thin

103

Page 104

Fun with Words

Look at the letters on the balloons. Use the letters to make the spelling words.

chop   this   them

check   then   that

Words Across the Curriculum

Say each math word. Trace each word. Then, write each word.

math   chart   much

math   chart   much

Write the math word that ends like **with**.   math

Write the math word that ends like **rich**.   much

104

Page 105

Words in Writing

Write directions telling how you do something. Use at least three words from the box.

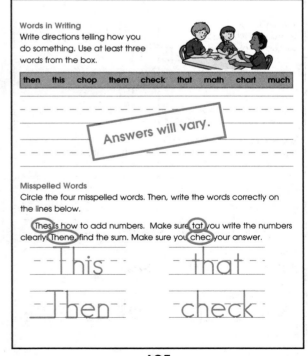

| then | this | chop | them | check | that | math | chart | much |

Answers will vary.

Misspelled Words

Circle the four misspelled words. Then, write the words correctly on the lines below.

Thes is how to add numbers. Make sure tat you write the numbers clearly. Thene, find the sum. Make sure you chec your answer.

This   that

Then   check

105

Answer Key

Spelling Words
Say each word. Listen to the beginning sound. trace each word. Write the word.

when   when
show   show
what   what
ship   ship
which   which
shut   shut

106

Words in Context
Write the missing spelling words.

What did you do last summer?

I sailed on a ship, where I had my own room. I could shut the door. When we go to the shore, I will show you which boat I was on.

Word Building
Add the letters **wh** to make words that ask questions. Remember, sentences start with a capital letter.

Who?   Why?
Where?

107

Fun with Words
Finish the spelling words to solve the puzzle.

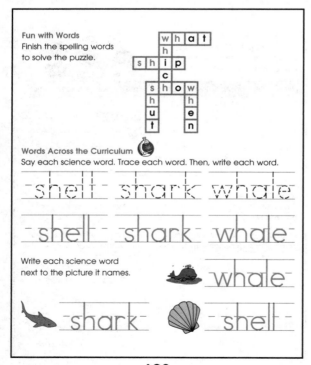

Words Across the Curriculum
Say each science word. Trace each word. Then, write each word.

shell   shark   whale
shell   shark   whale

Write each science word next to the picture it names.

whale
shark   shell

108

Words in Writing
Write about a trip you would like to make on a ship. Use at least three words from the box.

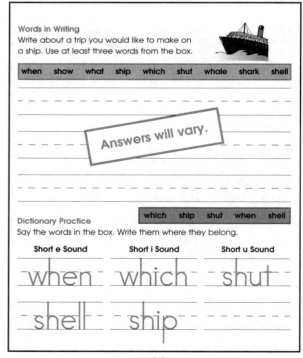

| when | show | what | ship | which | shut | whale | shark | shell |

Answers will vary.

Dictionary Practice

| which | ship | shut | when | shell |

Say the words in the box. Write them where they belong.

Short e Sound	Short i Sound	Short u Sound
when	which	shut
shell	ship	

109

Answer Key

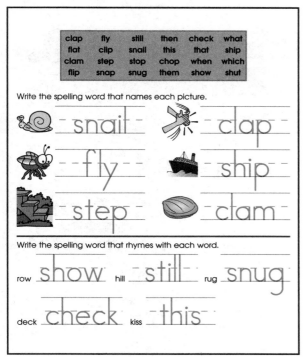

clap	fly	still	then	check	what
flat	clip	snail	this	that	ship
clam	step	stop	chop	when	which
flip	snap	snug	them	show	shut

Write the spelling word that names each picture.

snail   clap

fly   ship

step   clam

Write the spelling word that rhymes with each word.

row show   hill still   rug snug

deck check   kiss this

110

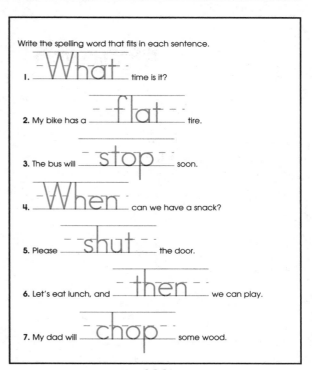

Write the spelling word that fits in each sentence.

1. What time is it?

2. My bike has a flat tire.

3. The bus will stop soon.

4. When can we have a snack?

5. Please shut the door.

6. Let's eat lunch, and then we can play.

7. My dad will chop some wood.

111

Words in Context
Write the missing spelling words.

My friend wrote me a note today. She

wants me to go to her home

after school. We can jump rope and play games.

hope my mom won't say no !

Word Building
Write o and e to make a word
that names each picture.

stove   pole

robe

112

Words in Context
Write the missing spelling words.

When I get up every day , I make

my bed the way my mom showed me to do it.

Then, I have breakfeast. Today, I ate eggs and

ham. I gave my dog a bite

of ham. Her name is Kate.

Word Building
Write a and e or ay to make a
word that names each picture.

cake

hay   gate

113

Answer Key

Fun with Words
Use the letters on the blocks to write the spelling words.

ate   gave   name

day   make   way

Words Across the Curriculum
Say each art word. Trace each word. Then, write each word.

clay   same   shape

clay   same   shape

Write the missing art words.

You can roll ___clay___ into the ___shape___ of a ball.

You can make another one that is the ___same___ size.

114

Words in Writing
Write about something you like to make.
Use at least three words from the box.

| make | day | way | clay | same |
| name | gave | ate | shape | |

Answers will vary.

Dictionary Practice
Write the spelling words in ABC order.

| make | day | way |
| name | gave | ate |

1. ate   3. day   5. gave

2. make   4. name   6. way

115

Spelling Words
Say each word. Listen for the long **i** sound. Trace each word. Write the word.

| **Spelling Tip** | These letter patterns can make the long **i** sound: **i-consonant-e** and **y**. |

like   like

time   time

kite   kite

my   my

ride   ride

by   by

116

Words in Context
Write the missing spelling words.

Mike is ___my___ best friend. We ___like___ to ___ride___ our bikes. One ___time___, we rode ___by___ the park. We saw a boy flying a ___kite___.

Word Building
Write **i** and **e** or **y** to make a word that names each picture.

dime

vine   fry

117

Spectrum Spelling
Grade 1
176

Answer Key

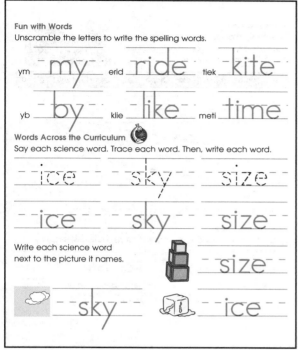

Fun with Words

Unscramble the letters to write the spelling words.

ym   **my**   erid   **ride**   tiek   **kite**

yb   **by**   klie   **like**   meti   **time**

Words Across the Curriculum

Say each science word. Trace each word. Then, write each word.

ice   sky   size

ice   sky   size

Write each science word next to the picture it names.

size

sky   ice

118

Words in Writing

Write about a shopping trip. Use at least three words from the box.

like	kite	ride	ice	size
time	my	by	sky	

Answers will vary.

Misspelled Words

Circle the four misspelled words. Then, write the words correctly on the lines below.

The last (tyme) went for a drive with (mi) mom, I did not (lik) it. We got a flat tire on one side of the car. I had to wait (bie) the car while she fixed it.

time   my

like   by

119

Spelling Words

Say each word. Listen for the long **o** sound. Write the word.

Spelling Tip   These letter patterns can make the long **o** sound: **o-consonant-e**, and **o**.

no   no

home   home

rope   rope

note   note

hope   hope

go   go

120

Words in Context

Write the missing spelling words.

My friend wrote me a **note** today. She

wants me to **go** to her **home**

after school. We can jump **rope** and play games. I

hope my mom won't say **no** .

Word Building

Write **o** and **e** to make a word that names each picture.

stove   pote   robe

121

Answer Key

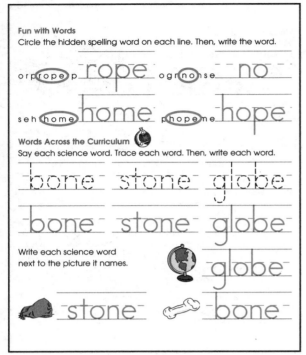

Fun with Words
Circle the hidden spelling word on each line. Then, write the word.

o r p (rope) p   rope   o g r n (no) s e   no

s e h (home) t   home   p (hope) n e   hope

Words Across the Curriculum
Say each science word. Trace each word. Then, write each word.

bone   stone   globe

bone   stone   globe

                 globe

Write each science word
next to the picture it names.

stone   bone

122

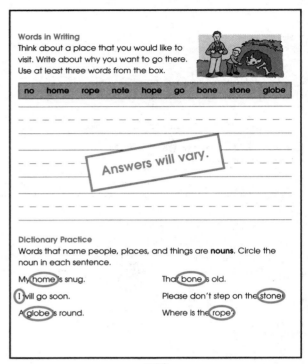

Words in Writing
Think about a place that you would like to visit. Write about why you want to go there. Use at least three words from the box.

| no | home | rope | note | hope | go | bone | stone | globe |

Answers will vary.

Dictionary Practice
Words that name people, places, and things are **nouns**. Circle the noun in each sentence.

My (home) is snug.   That (bone) is old.

I will (go) soon.   Please don't step on the (stone)

A (globe) is round.   Where is the (rope)?

123

Spelling Words
Say each word. Listen for the long **e** sound. Trace each word. Write the word.

| Spelling Tip | These letter patterns can make the long **e** sound: **e**, and **ee**. |

he   he

see   see

feet   feet

me   me

bee   bee

feet   feet

124

Words in Context
Write the missing spelling words.

My friend Lee is walking with ___me___

___He___ doesn't ___see___ what is

near his ___feet___. It is a ___bee___! If it

stings him, it will not ___feel___ good.

Word Building
Write **ee** to make a word that names each picture.

tree

peel   jeep

125

Answer Key

Page 126

Fun with Words
Use the letters in the leaves to make the spelling words.

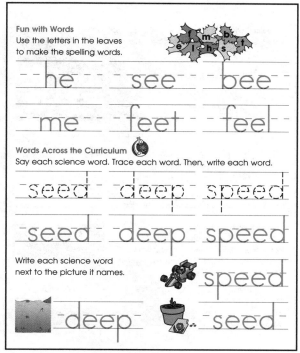

he   see   bee

me   feet   feel

Words Across the Curriculum
Say each science word. Trace each word. Then, write each word.

seed   deep   speed

seed   deep   speed

Write each science word next to the picture it names.

deep   speed

seed

126

Page 127

Words in Writing
Write about something you like to do outside. Use at least two words from the box.

| he | see | feet | me | bee | feel | speed | deep | seed |

Answers will vary.

Misspelled Words
Circle the misspelled word in each row. Then, write the word correctly.

me   bee   (se)   see

feet   (dep)   he   deep

speed   weed   (fel)   feet

127

Page 128

make	way	kite	no	hope	feet
name	ate	my	home	go	me
day	like	ride	rope	he	bee
gave	time	by	note	see	feel

Write the spelling word that names each picture.

rope   home

bee   feet

Write the two spelling words that rhyme with each word.

| why | hay | so |

by   way   go

my   day   no

128

Page 129

Read each word. Write the two spelling words that have the same beginning sound.

rip   ride   rope

mop   make   me

Write the spelling word that belongs in each sentence.

We ___ate___ ham and eggs.

I ___gave___ my mom a kiss.

Do you ___like___ to ride a bike?

What is your dog's ___name___?

129

Answer Key

Spelling Words
Say each word. Trace each word. Then, write the word.

the   the

are   are

for   for

was   was

said   said

you   you

130

Words in Context
Write the missing spelling words.

I __was__ late for __the__ party!

"__You__ must hurry," said __said__ my mom.

Your friends __are__ waiting __for__ you.

Word Building
A **contraction** is two words joined into one shorter word. Look at the contractions in the box. Then, write the contractions where they belong.

are not = aren't
was not = wasn't
you are = you're

was not	you are	are not
wasn't	you're	aren't

131

Fun with Words
Match the beginning letter of each spelling word with the rest of its letters.

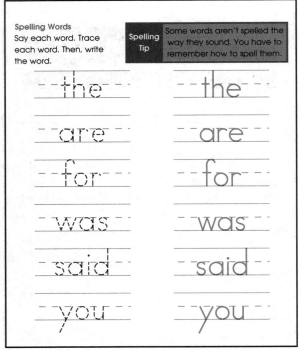

Words Across the Curriculum
Say each math word. Trace each word. Then, write each word.

add   many   all

add   many   all

Write each math word below its meaning.

every one	a lot	sum
all	many	add

132

Words in Writing
Write about a time when you have to count things. Use at least three words from the box.

the	for	said	add	all
are	was	you	many	

Answers will vary.

Dictionary Practice
Write the spelling words in ABC order.

the	for	said
are	was	you

1. are   3. for   5. said

2. the   4. was   6. you

133

Answer Key

Spelling Words
Say each word. Trace each word. Then, write the word.

Spelling Tip	Some words aren't spelled the way they sound. You have to remember how to spell them.

do   do
have   have
come   come
her   her
they   they
want   want

134

Words in Context
Write the missing spelling words.

I ___have___ two friends who ___want___ to play. I'll ask Mom if I need to ___do___ some work first. Then, I'll ask ___her___ if ___they___ can ___come___ over.

Word Building
Add **s** to tell what a boy is doing.

I ride. He rides.

I make. He make **s**.   I want. He want **s**.

I like. He like **s**.   I see. He see **s**.

135

Fun with Words
Circle the hidden spelling words.

r	w	a	n	t	c	p
t	r	e	c	d	o	t
n	k	o	c	e	m	h
t	r	h	a	v	e	e
h	e	r	w	d	e	y

Words Across the Curriculum
Say each math word. Trace each word. Then, write each word.

and   some   here
and   some   here

Write the missing letter to complete each math word.

some

here   and

136

Words in Writing
Do you like people to visit you at home? Write about your favorite visitors. Use at least three words from the box.

do	come	they	and	here
have	her	want	some	

Answers will vary.

Misspelled Words
Circle the word in each pair that is not spelled correctly.

they   (thay)   (cume)   come
(dou)   do   (hur)   her
have   (hav)   want   (wonte)

137

Answer Key

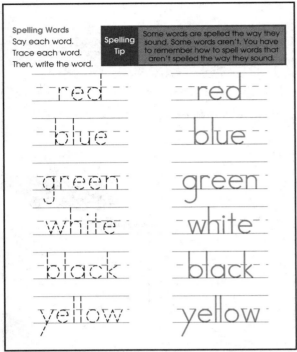

Spelling Words
Say each word.
Trace each word.
Then, write the word.

Spelling Tip Some words are spelled the way they sound. Some words aren't. You have to remember how to spell words that aren't spelled the way they sound.

red red
blue blue
green green
white white
black black
yellow yellow

138

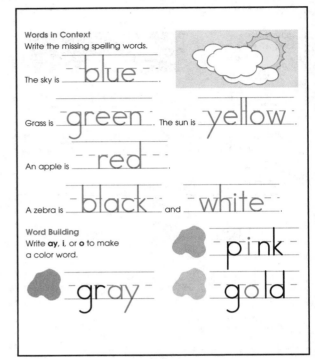

Words in Context
Write the missing spelling words.

The sky is blue

Grass is green. The sun is yellow

An apple is red.

A zebra is black and white.

Word Building
Write **ay**, **i**, or **o** to make a color word.

gray

pink

gold

139

Fun with Words
Write each color word where it belongs.

black yellow
green blue

Words Across the Curriculum
Say each art word. Then, write each word.

purple orange brown
purple orange brown

Write each art word next to the picture it names.

purple
brown orange

140

Words in Writing
What do different colors make you think of? Write about the colors of some things. Use at least three words from the box.

| red | green | black | purple | brown |
| blue | white | yellow | orange | |

Answers will vary.

Dictionary Practice
Write the spelling word that has each vowel sound listed below.

Short a Sound	Long e Sound	Long i Sound
black	green	white

141

Spectrum Spelling
Grade 1

Answer

182

Answer Key

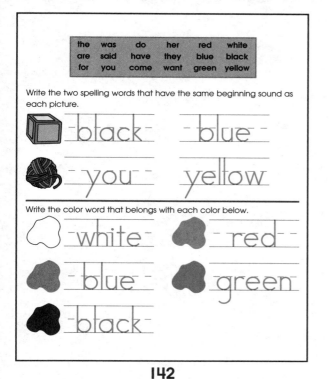

142

143